FIXING IMMIGRATION IN AMERICA

A COMMON SENSE PLAN FOR IMMIGRATION REFORM

ROBERT COUGHLON, JR.

Lucky 23 Media

Published by Lucky 23 Media, Phoenix, Arizona

robertcoughlon.com

Fixing Immigration in America:
A Common Sense Plan for Immigration Reform

ISBN 979-8-9959524-1-1 (paperback)
ISBN 979-8-9959524-0-4 (eBook)
Library of Congress Control Number: 2026918548

Publication managed by AuthorImprints.com

Table of Contents

Preface

MY WIFE KIM HAD THE idea that I should write this book as a guide for Americans on how we can change the immigration laws. The primary intended audience is native-born U.S. citizens. For some readers who are already familiar with immigration reform ideas, this book might be preaching to the choir. For others who may need some convincing, this book makes the case for why we need to change the immigration laws and exactly where we can meet in the middle. Above all, my lofty goal for this book is to bring Americans together and make America better.

I am inspired by my fellow immigration lawyers who dedicate themselves to advocating on behalf of immigrants and their families. As many practitioners will recognize, some of the ideas in this book are well-known and widely circulated, such as Section 249, the elimination of the 3 & 10 year bars, and an independent Immigration Court. Ira Kurzban, one of the most well-respected immigration lawyers in the country, has spent decades advocating for immigration reform, along with organizations such as Immigrants List, American Immigration Lawyers Association (AILA), American Immigration Council, and National Immigration Project.

Many of the ideas presented in this book are the brainchild of Mr. Kurzban and these outstanding organizations.

This book also presents bipartisan ideas from bills already proposed in Congress by both Republican and Democratic lawmakers, such as the American Dream and Promise Act, the Farm Workforce Modernization Act, the Dignity Act, and the Essential Workers for Economic Advancement Act, all of which are important parts of the conversation.

A few of the ideas are my own. "A Plan For ICE" is a synthesis of well-publicized ICE reform proposals with my own spin on it to bring back the Immigration and Naturalization Service. My idea for the "50-mile Rule" for interior immigration stops ("Kavanaugh stops") came about when I was thinking about how we could balance the need for border security with the need for sanity.

To make these ideas a reality, we must elect lawmakers who are willing to step away from partisanship and work together for the common good of the American people. I hope that everyone who reads this book will support the Immigrants List organization to help elect representatives who will finally get the job done.

My wife not only had the vision for this book, she has also been instrumental in making it happen. Many nights when I came home from the office, she would ask me, "Are you writing tonight?" This gave me the freedom to take the time to do it while also subtly reminding me that she expected to see progress. Procrastination wasn't an option. She also made countless intangible contributions to this book with our frequent conversations about everything going on in the world of immigration in the United States. She is my biggest cheerleader, and she made it easy to keep moving forward.

I want to thank my parents and my brother and sisters for all their support. Of course, I want to thank my kids Sarah, Matt, Claire, Kristen, and Kyle, who inspire and motivate me. I also want to thank my friends who have encouraged me over the years, especially a couple of my oldest friends from high school, Ron Antonette and Nick Hoffman.

I would also like to say, “Thank You,” to my clients. I have worked as an immigration lawyer for over 30 years, and I am grateful for the opportunity to be part of their immigration journeys.

I also appreciate the assistance of my editor, Ann Klefstad, for her feedback and invaluable help in polishing the manuscript.

Finally, I want to thank my friend and fellow immigration lawyer David Asser who told me I should be a writer.

It should be noted that although this book’s plan for immigration reform draws on ideas from many people, those individuals and organizations may not necessarily endorse every proposal presented in these pages.

Thank you all!

July 4, 2026
Robert Coughlon, Jr.

INTRODUCTION

Common Ground

PRESIDENT ABRAHAM LINCOLN described immigration as a "source of national wealth and strength." When he made that statement to Congress in 1863, Lincoln was both looking back and recognizing the many contributions of past immigrants and also foreshadowing how future immigrants would continue to build the United States in the coming years.

It is in this spirit that I invite you to read this book about immigration law in the United States, to learn about what the current law is, some of its history, and how our country would benefit from changing the law. This book could be seen as a vision for the future of immigration law in the United States, as a legal framework for how the U.S. can continue to be a nation of immigrants. I wrote this book with the hope that U.S. citizens will find it educational, written in a way that is understandable to people without prior legal knowledge. And for people who are already familiar with our current immigration law, I hope that this book will offer you new ways to think about it.

This book tackles many different topics of immigration law that are relevant to the current events in the United States. For example, I explain why most undocumented immigrants in the U.S. (including Dreamers) are unable to legalize their status under the current immigration law and what I believe would be a reasonable solution. There are also discussions about border security, legal immigration, and the Immigration Court, as areas where we could change the law. In addition, I offer a plan to reform ICE with proposed new rules for civil immigration law enforcement. The final chapter brings it all together and presents the practical benefits for ordinary Americans if we enact the immigration law changes proposed in this book.

About Me

I am an immigration lawyer. In my 30-plus years of practicing immigration law, I have primarily represented immigrants in family-based immigration cases, naturalization, and deportation defense in immigration court. More recently, starting in 2025, I began doing federal court habeas corpus litigation, as well. My experience as a lawyer has given me a unique insight into the problems with the current immigration law, and what we can do to fix it.

Even as a child, I always had an interest in immigration because of my father. My dad had been in the Air Force in the mid-1960s. After he got out, he became a Border Patrol officer in California. Then, when I was a kid in the 1970s, he worked for the Immigration and Naturalization Service in Los Angeles. During that time, my dad went to law school at night. After he graduated, he passed the California bar exam and became an immigration lawyer. Throughout my high school and college years, I saw him representing people in different immigration contexts, applying for green cards, going to immigration court, and representing businesses in business-related immigration cases. I could see that my dad was helping people and that his clients were very appreciative. This contributed to my positive outlook about immigrants and immigration in general.

When I became an attorney in 1993, I gravitated toward being an immigration lawyer myself, first working for my dad and eventually going out on my own.

My dad practiced immigration law for twenty-five years. Then, he retired from his law practice so that he and my mom could move closer to their grandkids. Not long after, he went back to work for the government, this time as an attorney for the Department of Homeland Security, and then he became an Immigration Judge at the age of 67. After 8 years on the bench, he retired from the Immigration Court in 2019.

In my career as an immigration lawyer, I have only represented immigrants and I have never worked for the government. But my father's influence has undoubtedly caused me to look at immigration law from all sides. I hope that this book reflects a balanced perspective on immigration law and how we can change it for the better.

CHAPTER 1

But First, How We Got Here

A Brief History of U.S. Immigration Law

LET'S TALK ABOUT HOW IMMIGRATION worked in the "good ol' days." Prior to 1921, the U.S. mostly had an open-borders policy. If you wanted to come to the U.S., you just had to find a way to get here. According to the USCIS website, "Americans encouraged relatively free and open immigration during the 18th and early 19th centuries, and rarely questioned that policy until the late 1800s." In the latter part of the 19th century and throughout the 20th century, the United States made many changes to the immigration laws, leading up to the 1996 Illegal Immigration Reform and Immigrant Responsibility Act (IIRIRA). The U.S. has changed the immigration laws so many times because we keep trying to get it right. Changing the immigration laws is as American as baseball and apple pie. In 2026, we find ourselves still saddled with the 1996 law, which has turned out not to work for the benefit of U.S. citizens as advertised, and has arguably given rise to waste and abuse by our own government. So, it's time to change the law again.

A History of Change

Prior to 1921, if you were European, able-bodied, without obvious, disqualifying physical or mental health issues, you got in. All you had to do was buy a ticket on a ship. So, if that was your ancestor, doing it "the right way" literally meant "just do it." They didn't have to ask for permission or a visa to get on the ship. When they got off the ship, they had to get a health check and not look like they were going to need assistance.

My great-great grandfather David Sarsfield Coughlon was born in County Cork, Ireland, in 1848. He was brought to the United States as a child by his mother during the famine in Ireland, in 1854. They did it "the right way," which meant that they sailed to New York and, when they arrived, they gave the government officials their names. That was pretty much it. At the age of 25, David Sarsfield married Lena, age 19, who was born in Illinois, but whose parents had immigrated from Ireland. David and Lena were Irish Catholics, and they moved to Iowa where they farmed the land and raised a large family.

On my mom's side of the family, my grandmother was born in Italy in 1920 and arrived in the United States on May 24, 1921. My grandmother was brought to the U.S. as a baby by her mother, travelling to West Virginia to join my grandmother's father, who had come a year earlier to work as a coal miner. They, too, did it "the right way," for that time, which did not require much more than buying passage on the ship.

Many of our ancestors benefitted from far less restrictive immigration laws than we have today. So stating that someone did it "the right way" over a hundred years ago is really just to say that they were able to take advantage of the open border policy that existed up until 1921.

There was a tremendous wave of 25 million immigrants that began around 1880 and lasted until 1921. And there was a corresponding backlash: some Americans already here pushed back against those immigrants. The Americans whose ancestors had already come to America before that time were mostly white Anglo-Saxon Protestants who believed they were "natives" of the United States and that the Italians and others from southern or eastern Europe were the unskilled and dirty people, with different languages and different cultures. These nativists believed that America belonged to the White race because they got here first.

By 1921, this "nativism" grew to an extent that propelled Congress to pass the Emergency Quota Act of 1921 on May 19, 1921, in order to stop the great wave of immigration that America had been experiencing for the past 40 years—from 1880 to 1920. The Emergency Quota Act of 1921 put a limit on the number of immigrants the U.S. would accept each year, at 350,000 per year, and the law also capped the number of immigrants from any particular country at 3 percent of the number of residents already here from that country as of the 1910 census. But the Emergency Quota Act of 1921 was a quick fix. In 1924, Congress passed an even more restrictive immigration law, called the 1924 Immigration Act, which limited the annual number of immigrants to 165,000 per year, and sharply limited immigration from the countries of the most recent immigrants. In addition, the 1924 Immigration Act practically eliminated any further immigration from Asia.

The 1924 Immigration Act's quota system did not apply to countries in the Western Hemisphere. This meant that, although there were numerical limits on southern European countries and an outright ban on Asians, there were no numerical limits on the number of Mexicans, Canadians, or other people from Western Hemisphere countries.

In 1929, Congress passed the Registry Act of 1929, which created a legal process for the government to create an official arrival record for people who had lived in the U.S. continuously since the cutoff date of June 3, 1921, and were of good moral character, but who did not have any record of being admitted. This was, in effect, the first "legalization program" in the United States.

To recognize Americans' anxiety over immigration in the early 20th century is not an indictment of them in general. Rather, it merely shows that human beings sometimes have knee-jerk reactions to sudden changes in demographics, and those reactions fail to recognize the many contributions of the newcomers. For example, during World War II, immigrants and their sons and daughters and grandchildren were some of the heroes of the Greatest Generation. More than 300,000 foreign-born individuals served in the U.S. Army during World War II, and more than 109,000 foreign-born members of the U.S. Armed Forces became naturalized citizens between July 1942 and June 1945.

In 1942, there was a U.S. agricultural labor shortage caused by World War II. In response, the U.S. and Mexico created the Bracero Program, which brought Mexican migrants, most of whom were men, to the U.S. to do agricultural work. The Bracero Program started with an executive order, but it was later codified by Congress in 1951. The Bracero Program continued until 1964. During that time, millions of Mexican migrant workers came to the U.S. to provide agricultural labor and to fuel the U.S. economy. The Bracero Program provided a much-needed legal guest-worker system for the U.S. to bring in migrant labor, but it also created its own problems, such as low wages for farm workers and poor working conditions.

In 1952, Congress passed the 1952 Immigration and Nationality Act, which repealed the Asian exclusion laws and eliminated race as a barrier to naturalization. This was an important step in the right direction. But it also kept in place the 1924 national-origins quota systems.

The 1952 Act also gave us one of the most important and long-lasting benefits of modern U.S. immigration law, Section 245(a), commonly known as "adjustment of status." Congress's invention of adjustment of status has become the legal mechanism that many Americans now take for granted: that many immigrants can stay in the U.S. while they go through the immigration process without having to leave. This concept allows a noncitizen who qualifies for an immigrant visa and who is already inside the U.S. to be able to apply for lawful permanent residence without having to go back to their home country and apply for an immigrant visa at a U.S. consulate to then reenter as a permanent resident. This section of the law has become vital to ensure continuity in the lives of U.S. citizens married to foreign-born spouses. It also allows foreign workers who are here legally to be able to stay in the U.S. while they apply for their green cards. Adjustment of status is a great example of how Congress changed the law to respond to Americans' need and desire for immigrants. However, adjustment of status under Section 245(a) is only available for someone who had entered the U.S. with a visa (Section 245(a) cannot be used by undocumented immigrants who entered the U.S. without a visa).

One of the shortcomings of the 1952 law, though, was that it kept in place the discriminatory national-origins quota system from 1924, a problem that was remedied in 1965 when Congress passed a new immigration law, the Immigration and Nationality Act of 1965, signed by President Lyndon Johnson. The 1965 law ended the 1924 national-origins test and implemented a new system for legal immigration which is still in place today. This basic framework for legal immigration prioritizes immigration based upon close family relationships ("family-based immigration") and employment skills ("employment-based immigration"). This is still the basic framework for legal immigration in the U.S.

However, in turn, one of the drawbacks of the 1965 law was that it failed to replace the Bracero Program with a realistic temporary worker program to meet the continued demand for migrant labor from Mexico. The result of this was that migrants continued to come to the U.S. to do much-needed labor, such as in agriculture and construction, but the law was too restrictive to meet the U.S. economy's demand for that migrant labor. The result was that the migrants continued to come to the U.S. to fill jobs, but there hasn't been any legal immigration system in place for them to "do it the right way."

In 1980, Congress passed the Refugee Act of 1980, which officially created the asylum and refugee laws in the United States. This law incorporated international humanitarian standards into our immigration law. For asylum seekers, this is the law that tells asylum officers and immigration judges which immigrants should be given protection.

After 1965, the U.S. population of long-term undocumented immigrants grew in large numbers. In 1986, Congress and President Reagan addressed this issue with the passage of the Immigration Reform and Control Act of 1986 (IRCA) which legalized the immigration status of long-term undocumented immigrants and some agricultural workers. Also, for the first time in history, it penalized hiring undocumented migrants.

In 1990, President Bush signed the Immigration Act of 1990 which expanded legal immigration. For example, this law increased the number of employment-based immigrant visas from 54,000 per year to 140,000 per year. It also added Temporary Protected Status to allow the Attorney General to protect people from deportation who were from designated countries experiencing civil war, natural disasters, or some other extraordinary temporary conditions.

Illegal Immigration Reform and Immigrant Responsibility Act of 1996 (IIRIRA)

The last time Congress actually passed immigration law reform (not just a border security bill or a spending bill), signed into law by a President, was 1996. This law, called the Illegal Immigration Reform and Immigrant Responsibility Act of 1996 (IIRIRA), was signed by President Clinton. IIRIRA was meant to crack down on illegal immigration at the border, in the workplace, and in the criminal justice system. IIRIRA has been in place for the last 30 years, and it's responsible for the mess we're in right now.

Here are some examples of how this law makes it practically impossible for many immigrants to "do it the right way."

First, let's remember that under Section 245(a) (dating back to 1952) if a noncitizen entered the United States without inspection by an immigration officer ("crossing the border illegally"), then they're generally not eligible to fix their immigration status inside the U.S. without leaving and applying for a visa at a U.S. consulate or embassy abroad. So, for those immigrants to fix their immigration status, they would have to go back to their country and apply for a visa to re-enter. This worked up until 1996. But in 1996 with IIRIRA, Congress created something called the "10 year bar," formally known as the INA Section 212(a)(9)(B). It says that if a person came to the U.S. illegally and stayed for more than one year, after turning 18, then leaves the U.S. for any reason (such as to apply for a visa to come back legally) then they're not eligible to get a visa or green card for 10 years, unless they qualify for a waiver (which many people don't qualify for and, if they do, is difficult to obtain and also takes years). I suppose that when legislators wrote this law they envisioned that all of the immigrants who had come illegally and stayed for more than a year would go back to their home country and wait there for 10 years to be allowed back into the U.S. But it backfired on them. What actually happened is that the 10 year bar is so unbearable (for a person to leave their family for 10 years) that people are not able to complete the legal immigration process. At the time IIRIRA became law—1996 and going forward—if someone had come illegally and stayed for more than a year, it became practically impossible to "do it the right way" because leaving the life you'd built in the U.S. to go back and start over in your home country with no job prospects was too much to expect.

In practical effect, this law serves to disqualify people, even if they are eligible to apply for a green card through a family relationship or job offer. Just by leaving the U.S. to go to the U.S. consulate in their home country to apply for a visa and "do it the right way," they "trigger the bar" and can't come back for 10 years. The effect of the 10-year bar is that people who have come to the U.S. illegally and stayed for more than a year are trapped here... because to leave would be to abandon their family and life in the U.S. This is just one of the most glaring examples of how the immigration system is broken because of IIRIRA. There seems no reason to preserve this impracticable and overly burdensome requirement.

Another example of how hard IIRIRA is on immigrants is the section known as "Cancellation of Removal." This is the section that is supposed to be a waiver that an immigration judge can grant for people who have lived in the U.S. for more than 10 years, are of good moral character, aren't criminals, and who have a child, a spouse, or a parent who is either a U.S. citizen or lawful permanent resident (referred to as a "qualifying relative"). But there's one more requirement that's the kicker, that makes it almost impossible for most people to qualify. The law says that the immigration judge can only grant the case if the person's qualifying relative (such as their child, spouse, or parent) would suffer "exceptional and extremely unusual hardship" if the person gets deported. And the law says that all the immigration judges in the whole country can only grant up to 4,000 cases per year in total, for Cancellation of Removal for Non-Permanent Residents. "Exceptional and extremely unusual hardship" is a very high bar that most immigrants can't meet. The effect of this is that, for a person to have a chance of winning their Cancellation of Removal case, the qualifying relative usually needs to have some serious condition that would not receive proper treatment in the country where the U.S. citizen would be going to be with their relative who got deported. On the other hand, if it's a regular family where one or both of the parents is undocumented and the kids are U.S. citizens, and the kids are pretty typical American kids, the law says that person doesn't qualify for his or her deportation to be "cancelled" and get to stay here because the hardship is "ordinary" and not "exceptional and extremely unusual."

Not long after IIRIRA was signed by President Clinton, it was apparent to a lot of people that the immigration system was broken, but it never got fixed. President George W. Bush talked about immigration reform, but he didn't get it done. In 2006, under Bush, the Senate passed the Comprehensive Immigration Reform Act which combined tougher immigration enforcement with a path to legal status for undocumented immigrants who had lived in the U.S. for a long time. But the House had much different ideas, and they passed a bill that was all about deporting people. The Senate and the House were not able to agree on a final bill, so nothing happened.

President Obama probably could have fixed the immigration laws during the first two years of his first term when the Democrats controlled the House and the Senate, but immigration took a backseat to health care. Then after those first two years, the balance of parties in Congress changed and the opportunity was lost. In 2013, under Obama, the "Gang of Eight" comprehensive immigration bill passed the Senate. This bill, called the Border Security, Economic Opportunity, and Immigration Modernization Act, would have legalized undocumented immigrants who had lived here for many years and would have beefed up immigration enforcement. But the House was controlled by Republicans, and the Republican Speaker of the House killed it by never bringing it for a vote.

President Trump's first term as President was devoted almost entirely to immigration enforcement. At the time President Trump took office in 2017, there was an emerging border crisis with increasing numbers of undocumented border crossers. President Trump responded to this as a way to show strength, in two major ways. First, he punished people who crossed the border illegally by separating children from their parents as a deterrent to others who might try to bring their children to the U.S. This resulted in untold trauma to children who were forcibly separated from their parents for years before the government reunited them. President Trump also attempted to stem the tide of asylum seekers by instituting a policy called "Remain in Mexico," where asylum seekers at the southern border had to physically stay in Mexico while trying to apply for asylum in the U.S. This was also inhumane because it shut the door on asylum seekers, who often had no means of support in Mexico and who were seeking asylum, of course, because they were in danger in their home country. There was great public disapproval of these policies.

In terms of attempts to substantively change the immigration laws during President Trump's first term, in February 2018, the Senate put up four different immigration reform bills for a vote, but none of them got enough votes to overcome a filibuster and advance. Also under President Trump in his first term, the House passed the American Dream and Promise Act twice, which would have given permanent status to immigrants who were brought here as kids. During the same time, the House also passed the Farm Workforce Modernization Act which would have legalized undocumented immigrants and would have improved the H-2A temporary visa program for farmworkers. But these bills did not make it through the Senate. I believe these bills were examples of how the American public supported the idea that the border had become more secure under President Trump and that it was time to legalize the immigration status of those who were already here, and who had not committed crimes.

By the time President Biden was elected on November 3, 2020, there was a mood among most Americans that we should have immigration reform to legalize the immigration status of the millions of non-criminal immigrants who had already been living in the U.S. for many years but who had been unable to fix their status due to the impossible immigration laws on the books. But that general mood of optimism soon evaporated when an unprecedented number of people came to the southern border and it turned into a full-blown crisis. The Department of Homeland Security was ill-equipped to deal with the millions of asylum seekers because our immigration laws had not prepared for this type of situation. Whereas President Trump had separated children from their parents and told asylum seekers they couldn't come in, President Biden responded as a humanitarian but, in doing so, became known as the President who let a lot of immigrants in. And, of course, during President Biden's term, Congress couldn't agree on a bill. It must be noted that in the spring of 2024, it looked like Congress was going to pass the Secure Border Act (which President Biden would have gladly signed) but Donald J. Trump (who was running for President again) influenced the Republicans in Congress to not pass the bill because Mr. Trump wanted to use immigration as his most forceful selling point in the election that year.

Mr. Trump was indeed elected President in 2024 because Americans did not like what they saw as "an invasion" by migrants at the southern border during President Biden's term. The use of that term here is not an endorsement of that term or that characterization. But it is a reality that this sentiment influenced the 2024 election.

As of this writing, President Trump in two terms has spent enormous sums money on immigration enforcement but he has not led Congress to change the immigration laws. During President Trump's second term, there have been opportunities to improve the immigration laws, but the House and Senate have been slow to advance the proposed changes. One of the reasons for the House and Senate reluctance to act is because the current Administration has engaged in anti-immigrant propaganda to stir up hate against immigrants. This propaganda has demonized immigrants, especially those who came here without visas, by falsely casting them as criminals who vote illegally, take Americans' jobs, and somehow rely on public assistance. These myths just are not true. For example, of the hundreds of thousands of immigrants whom the government has arrested since January 2025, at least seventy percent of them do not have any criminal record at all.

The overwhelming majority of Americans agree that, by and large, immigration is a good thing and that we need comprehensive immigration reform to fix our broken immigration system. Even law-and-order Republicans, such as Sheriff Grady in Florida, have spoken up recently and called for immigration reform because we need a solution for the millions of people who are our friends and neighbors who have lived in the U.S. peacefully for many years, but have not been able to legalize their immigration status. For most of the undocumented immigrants living in the

United States, it's impossible for them obtain legal immigration status. It's not for lack of trying. They just don't qualify under the current law.

Do They Pay Their Fair Share?

There has been a lot of discussion about whether immigrants are a "drain" on government budgets. Some people think immigrants take more than they give, and other people think immigrants pay more into the system than they get back.

In February of 2026, the Cato Institute published a study about the budgetary effects of immigrants: "Immigrants' Recent Effects on Government Budgets: 1994-2023," authored by David J. Bier, Michael Howard, and Julián Salazar. The Cato Institute promotes largely libertarian ideas, neither liberal nor conservative: freedom, limited government, reduced government spending, lower taxes, and fewer regulations.

The study found that for the 30 years from 1994-2023, "the U.S. immigrant population generated more in taxes than they received in benefits from all levels of government." That means that, as a whole, immigrants paid more in taxes than they received in benefits. The study also found that for those 30 years "immigrants created a cumulative fiscal surplus of $14.5 trillion in real 2024 dollars." That means immigrants helped us pay off our debt. The authors of the study point out that government spending on the U.S. military, which is one of our largest budget items, would be the same with or without immigrants. Immigrants actually help pay for the military. Immigrants are a net positive. They pay in more than they take out, which means the extra money they pay in helps to pay for things we all enjoy, like national security.

Likewise, the study says that the average U.S. citizen also pays more in taxes than they receive in government benefits. But the study shows that immigrants actually contribute a higher *share* of taxes because a higher percentage of immigrants are employed than U.S. citizens. This is not a bad thing. Some U.S. citizens are unable to work for a variety of reasons and we should be glad that we have immigrants paying taxes.

This is not to say that immigrants don't use government benefits.

Immigrants use almost the same amount of government benefits, on average, as U.S. citizens. But undocumented immigrants, in particular, by and large are not eligible to use needs-based government programs such as Medicaid, food assistance, and unemployment insurance.

Very interestingly, the study found that for those 30 years, "immigrants were about half as likely to be incarcerated as the U.S.-born population." The immigrant share of the prison population was far lower than their share of the general population. U.S. citizens are more likely to be in prison than immigrants. This is not a knock against U.S. citizens. This is an illustration that immigrants as a group are just as good—as law-abiding—as U.S. citizens are as a group. They are equal to us in character.

Starting in 2025, the government, including its social media apparatus, has tried to make people think that "criminal aliens" are terrorizing our country, and that we need the government to protect us by deporting all undocumented immigrants. The government has told us, and they keep telling us, that they're going after the "worst of the worst." But they're not. Approximately seventy percent of the noncitizens that the government has arrested since January 20, 2025 have no criminal record at all.

The Immigration and Nationality Act uses the word "alien" to describe a person who is not a citizen or national of the United States, which is consistent with the original meaning of the word as simply a foreigner. But obviously this word has taken a modern meaning that refers to a nonhuman from a place other than Earth. So, although it is a word with legal significance under the immigration laws, to use it casually (especially with the additional adjective "criminal") to describe immigrants blurs the line between legal definition and propaganda.

On February 11, 2026, on social media, DHS posted four photographs of migrant groups at the southern border, possibly from the time between 2021-2024. The caption read: Remember what they did to our country.

Within hours, the post was flooded with comments. Most of the commenters said positive things about immigrants. Some of them are deeply poignant and insightful. The commenters recounted stories of the generosity and kindness of immigrants. Many people have stories of being invited into immigrants' homes, and many others have stories of immigrants saving their day. Also, many Americans are very thankful for all the hard work of immigrants doing difficult jobs. It is interesting that when the government posts pictures which it intended to show immigrants in a bad light, Americans respond by standing up for immigrants because immigrants are our family and friends.

Another of the popular lies told about immigrants is that they vote illegally. Illegal voting by noncitizen immigrants is largely a myth, and it is well-documented that it is a myth. Out of the hundreds of millions of votes cast in recent elections, there have been only a small handful of accusations of illegal voting by immigrants. The number is so infinitesimally small compared to the hundreds of millions of votes by U.S. citizens that it is statistically insignificant. These few instances did not influence election results at all. That's a fact.

As of 2026, passing a comprehensive immigration law that fixes all the problems with our current broken system is something no President has been able to do since it all became a mess in 1996. We hope that will change soon.

CHAPTER 2

Registry

MY DAD, WHO IS A retired immigration judge, always likes to say, “The easiest way to fix the immigration law would be to just update Section 249.” Section 249 is a section of the immigration law that already says that person can get a green card if they’ve been here for a certain period of time. But under the current law, a person has to have been in the U.S. since before January 1, 1972 to qualify. Obviously, this doesn’t help any immigrant who has come to the U.S. in the last 54 years.

Updating Section 249 is not a new idea. Plenty of people have thought of it before and suggested it. I have been told that my immigration lawyer friends David Asser and Mo Goldman wrote a memo about updating Section 249 and gave it as a suggestion to a representative of then-Secretary of Homeland Security Janet Napolitano under President Obama. But Secretary Napolitano never contacted them and, of course, President Obama did not accomplish immigration reform.

Updating Section 249 is exactly the plan that Senator Alex Padilla has proposed in his bill, Renewing Immigration Provisions of the Immigration Act of 1929, which he introduced on July 28, 2025.

In 1929, Congress passed an immigration law that allowed people who had come to the U.S. prior to June 3, 1921 to become lawful permanent residents and get their "green cards," even though there was no record of their entry into the country. The 1929 law said that the government should "register" immigrants who lived in the United States but could not prove that they had come legally. The law said that the government should write down the names of all the people who had been living here since at least June 3, 1921, and who didn't have proof of how they entered the U.S., and make those people lawful permanent residents, as long as they weren't criminals or had done something else that would disqualify them. The original registry date (the "cutoff" date) was June 3, 1921. The idea behind Section 249 was that if an immigrant didn't have a record of a legal entry into the U.S., but was a good person who hadn't committed a crime or done something that would get them deported, then the government should just put their names on the list of people who are lawfully admitted for permanent residence. In the 1929 law, Congress instructed the government to grant these individuals lawful permanent resident status.

This process in the law has been on the books for almost 100 years. Over the years, Congress has tinkered with it a little bit here and there, and has extended the "registry date" five different times. The last time, though, was 1986. In 1986, President Reagan signed the Immigration Reform and Control Act of 1986, and it changed the cutoff date to January 1, 1972. That was the last update: forty years ago.

We could update Section 249 with a more recent "registry date," such as November 3, 2020, which is when Joe Biden was elected President. If we did this, undocumented immigrants and visa overstayers who came to the U.S. prior to November 3, 2020 would finally have an opportunity to "do it the right way." We could draw the line at Biden's election, so that the millions of people who came into the U.S. during his presidency will not benefit from this change.

Senator Padilla's bill would actually change the registry date from "January 1, 1972" to "living here for at least 7 years" (without a fixed date). There is a certain appeal to changing Section 249 so that the actual registry date is not fixed. This would make it so that in the future, someone would qualify if they had been here for at least 7 years, no matter when that time was. The argument for this type of change is that it prevents the law from becoming outdated again.

The entire point of updating Section 249 is to recognize there are people who have lived in the United States for decades without status and have established undeniable community ties. To sever these ties with them would actually harm the United States and our citizens. These folks are currently facing detention and deportation because the current immigration laws made it impossible for them to "do it the right way" in the first place and the law does not offer them any way to make amends now. There are both humanitarian and economic reasons for changing the immigration laws to legalize their status. We have millions of peaceful, hard-working undocumented immigrants in the United States who have spent many years building their lives in the U.S. This includes having kids born here who are United States citizens. These children and young adults are Americans who have every right to live in the United States themselves, and also understandably want for their parents to be able to remain here with them. Many of the millions of undocumented immigrants are now in their fifties and have not only adult U.S. citizen children, but also grandkids now. So, we need a solution that will allow these grandparents to continue to stay here with their grandkids while continuing to work and contribute to the economy of the United States.

Some of the undocumented immigrants have started businesses that Americans enjoy patronizing. Others have worked alongside native-born Americans in construction or farming. Many have already been paying income taxes and payroll taxes, which have helped to fund the federal government and Social Security. Legalization would bring all of them out of the shadows, so to speak, to become fully functioning participants in the United States economy. Updating Section 249 to legalize their status would recognize that they are deeply woven into the fabric of America and to deport them would harm the United States. For undocumented immigrants who have lived in the U.S. for many years peacefully, raising families, it is common sense that we should legalize their immigration status.

Like it or not, we need to have a law that provides a clear solution for people who came to the U.S. many years ago and have integrated into our society, but that also draws the line somewhere. There is also a political reality that updating Section 249 or any other legalization law requires a fixed cutoff date that does not include the recent arrivals. Although most Americans support legalization for longtime undocumented immigrants who haven't committed crimes, many Americans would be opposed to extending the same type of forgiveness to more recent arrivals who came seeking asylum.

If we have a registry date of November 3, 2020, for example, it would mean that if a person can prove they were in the U.S. on or before November 3, 2020, up until the date the law passes, they could register for lawful permanent residence. (This cutoff date does not negate the humanitarian concerns of those who came after. We should address their asylum claims separately and ensure that they are treated humanely and in compliance with our own Constitutional requirement of due process.) Additionally, by updating Section 249 and offering a legal solution for longtime undocumented immigrants, it would allow the Immigration Court to free up judicial resources to hear all the asylum cases of those who came after November 3, 2020.

Updating the Section 249 registry date to November 3, 2020, would change everything. It would give most undocumented immigrants here an opportunity to finally "do it the right way." Remember, up until now, most undocumented immigrants who have lived in the U.S. for the last 10 to 20 years haven't been able to "do it the right way" because it's impossible.

Forgiveness in Action

My favorite moment of Trump's presidency was when Kim Kardashian successfully lobbied for Alice Johnson's life sentence to be commuted. I thought President Trump showed great compassion for Alice Johnson. She had been sentenced to life imprisonment plus 5 years supervised release for her 1997 drug convictions; she had played a small part in a larger drug trafficking scheme. It was her first offense, and she was sentenced to life imprisonment.

Many people believed the federal criminal sentencing laws were too harsh. President Trump cited Alice Johnson as an example of this. Even if a person has been convicted of drug trafficking, they still deserve to be treated fairly. President Trump granted clemency to Johnson on June 6, 2018, which meant her time in prison was over and she walked out of prison as a free person, subject only to the other part of her sentence, 5 years of supervised release. Next, President Trump signed a criminal justice reform law called the First Step Act on December 21, 2018. He then later granted Alice Johnson a full pardon in 2020. I believe President Trump did the right thing when he commuted her sentence. She had already served over 20 years for having a small part in a big drug case.

So, what does this have to do with fixing immigration in the United States?

Let's go back to the fact that there are many Americans who look at undocumented immigrants and say, "They broke the law by coming here illegally." This is true. Under 8 U.S.C. Section 1325, titled "Improper entry by alien," it is a misdemeanor to enter the United States at a time or place not designated by immigration officers. Understandably, these Americans want there to be accountability for breaking the law by coming illegally.

Updating Section 249 would be like a pardon, except that most of the millions of undocumented immigrants who have been living in the United States since before November 3, 2020, were never charged with the crime of "Improper entry by alien," or any crime for that matter.

Is this amnesty? Amnesty is when the government gives a pardon to a large group of people. Pardons have become somewhat the norm recently, and it shouldn't be controversial to advocate that a group of otherwise law-abiding people, such as those who crossed the border illegally twenty years ago and who have never gotten into trouble with the police, should be pardoned for their transgression. Undocumented immigrants are just as worthy of a pardon as the folks who have already received pardons. The high moral ground on this issue is to be forgiving and forgetful of the wrongdoing and move on with life.

This would be an act of grace on the part of the United States. But it would also be limited to people who have good moral character. This means that they will have to be fingerprinted to be "vetted." A basic requirement would be to show good moral character. Therefore, the first step would be that people must come forward and be fingerprinted to show that they are people of good moral character who deserve forgiveness.

Make Them Earn It

But I'm actually not proposing that we simply give them a pardon without any accountability. There should be some sort of fine or payment to the United States, and possibly other requirements. For example, I would propose a fine in the amount of $3,000. This is a significant amount of money that shows accountability and appropriate restitution for either coming to the United States without a visa or overstaying a visa.

A similar proposal that has been made is the Dignity Act, a bill currently in Congress sponsored by Florida U.S. Representative Maria Salazar. The Dignity Act would give undocumented immigrants the opportunity to apply for "earned legalization" (which is different than applying for a green card under Section 249). This would provide legalization of their immigration status, but would not be lawful permanent residency (such as under Section 249). The requirements to qualify for earned legalization under the Dignity Act are actually pretty tough. A person would have to pay "restitution" to the United States government in the amount of $7,000 (to be paid over 7 years), plus learn English. It creates a number of hoops to jump through, which may not be realistic for all of the millions of undocumented immigrants. It's designed to be somewhat burdensome and require a great deal of effort and expense on the part of immigrants in order to meet all the requirements. If someone were to do all of these things, then the person would be going above and beyond to prove themself worthy. But still, they wouldn't be getting a green card. Rather, they would be getting a "Dignity" status with renewable work permit. Doing all of these things to attain legal status without a path to citizenship is far from a pardon.

And still, there are some politicians who don't like it because they think that doing anything at all to allow undocumented immigrants to become legal instead of being deported is amnesty. I guess they don't really want to fix the immigration problem we have in the U.S. They would rather just keep going down the road we're on, trying to coerce millions of hard-working people to leave, even though most Americans don't want their peaceful neighbor who is an undocumented immigrant to leave.

The Dignity Act represents a genuine effort to bring people together and positively change the immigration laws in a bipartisan way. On the earned legalization question, the Dignity Act really puts the onus on immigrants to earn it. Nothing is given to them under the Dignity Act. My concern about the Dignity Act is that, by creating so many hoops to jump through, it might be so rigorous that many of the intended recipients might not be able to fulfill all of the requirements, which would leave us in a place similar to where we are today. For example, encouraging immigrants to speak English is a laudable goal, but we already do that with naturalization. There is already an English language requirement for naturalization and there has never been such a requirement for lawful permanent residence, much less for work permits.

As it is, many immigrants already speak English with varying degrees of proficiency. But what would we do if an immigrant hasn't yet reached a certain level of English proficiency, but has paid the fine, has already been paying taxes, and qualifies in every other way? I don't think it makes sense to exclude good, hard-working people from legalization just because he or she hasn't been able to learn to speak English at the level of proficiency required. For these reasons, I don't think that having an English requirement for temporary, renewable Dignity status would be the right thing to do.

The Dignity Act requires the payment of back taxes, as well. I would propose that we require that immigrants submit their tax returns and proof of payment starting from 2020. After all, this is the critical year that we would be requiring proof that a person was in the United States. It would make sense that if the government is requiring proof that a person was here during that year, then the government should also require a tax return for that year and payment of taxes. I would propose that if the Dignity Act were to pass, then the requirement of back taxes would be to show tax returns and payments for each year starting in 2020. Many immigrants have been filing tax returns anyway, so it should not be a problem for them. For anyone who hasn't been filing tax returns, then this time period would be reasonable for them to file the returns and get on a payment plan, if necessary.

Perhaps the most important distinction between Section 249 Registry and an earned legalization program such as the Dignity Act is that Section 249 allows an immigrant to register to become a lawful *permanent* resident if they have lived in the U.S. for a certain period of time, whereas an earned legalization program such as the Dignity Act would offer an opportunity to apply for *temporary* legal status that is not lawful permanent residence and does not lead to U.S. citizenship. A lawful permanent resident (such as under Section 249) has the right to live in the United States for the rest of their life and can apply for U.S. citizenship after five years, whereas a person who has lawful temporary status under an earned legalization law would be able to stay as long as they renew it but would not have a path to citizenship. The Dignity Act would offer undocumented immigrants the opportunity to have: (1) protection from deportation; (2) the legal ability to work; and (3) the ability to legally travel in and out of the United States to finally visit family in their home countries whom they haven't seen in many years. Arguably, these pressing concerns are more important to undocumented immigrants than the possibility of future permanent residence or U.S. citizenship. This would offer them temporary legal status to remain here and work and be with their families, but that would not lead to the right to vote.

My Final Answer

My suggestion is that we combine some of the ideas behind the Dignity Act and apply them to Section 249. Here's a common sense, middle of the road solution:

Update the Registry date of Section 249 to November 3, 2020, but make it *conditional* lawful permanent residence for 10 years. Then, after 10 years of conditional lawful permanent residence, if they have paid taxes, stayed out of trouble and have not received public assistance, they can have the conditions removed to be an unrestricted lawful permanent resident. When undocumented immigrants come forward initially to register for the 10 year conditional LPR status, they would have to show good moral character, pay a $3,000 fine up-front, and be up-do-date on their tax returns since 2020.

Updating Section 249 Registry in this way would be a win-win for everybody. Registry would ensure that millions of undocumented immigrants are properly and thoroughly vetted. By giving undocumented immigrants a way to apply for conditional legal status, it would give them an opportunity to finally do it the right way, but also be accountable for entering the U.S. without a visa. They could continue to make financial contributions to our country through payment of income taxes and Social Security payroll taxes. Registry would keep families together and ensure that Americans continue to enjoy their presence here in the U.S. Plus, it would raise many billions of dollars to pay for additional border security.

My dad has told me that after President Trump was elected in 2024, he sent a letter to the President to suggest that they update Section 249 Registry. But apparently, my dad's letter has not yet made its way to the Resolute desk. My dad remains optimistic, though, that Congress will do the right thing and finally give millions of undocumented immigrants the ability to "do it the right way."

For immigration reform to be common sense, we have to draw the line somewhere. This means that the cutoff date for Registry should be November 3, 2020. A noncitizen must have been here before November 3, 2020, in order to qualify. Registry will be for the folks who have been here a long time and who have already made countless contributions to this country. This puts us back to where we were heading when Biden was elected, toward a more humanitarian view of immigrants.

CHAPTER 3

Dreamers

THERE IS A SUB-GROUP OF undocumented immigrants who have lived in the United States many years, known as "Dreamers." Dreamer usually refers to someone who was brought to the United States as a child many years ago. There are hundreds of thousands of immigrants who were born in another country and their parents or someone else brought them to the United States at a young age. Very few made this choice themselves. Someone else made the decision to bring them here, and then they grew up in the United States. They speak English and, for many of them, the United States is the only country they have ever known because they came at such a young age they have no recollection of their home country. Many of these folks are now well into adulthood, in their thirties and forties, and have established themselves in the same way as any person born in the U.S.

The DREAM Act was first introduced in Congress in 2001. The full name is the Development, Relief, and Education for Alien Minors (DREAM) Act. It has never been passed into law. In June, 2012, President Obama created Deferred Action for Childhood Arrivals (DACA). DACA was an executive action to give temporary protection from deportation (and work permits) to Dreamers. In order to qualify for DACA, a person must have (1) been physically present in the U.S. on June 15, 2012, (2) arrived in the United States prior to their 16th birthday, (3) continuously resided in the U.S. since June 15, 2007 (for at least 5 years prior to the announcement), (4) be under the age of 31 at the time of announcement on June 15, 2012, (5) either be enrolled in school, or completed high school, earned a GED, or be an honorably discharged veteran, and (6) not have a felony conviction, a significant misdemeanor, or 3 or more misdemeanors. In addition, a person had to be at least 15 years old in order to apply for DACA. Since 2012, there have been hundreds of thousands of DACA recipients. However, DACA did not provide a permanent solution and it does not provide a pathway to lawful permanent residence. In July 2021, due to federal court litigation, USCIS stopped processing new DACA applications, which meant that many Dreamers who had not yet turned 15 years old still have not been able to apply.

The United States is extremely lucky to have the 500,000 or so Dreamers we have here. Many have pursued higher education and they work in such jobs as doctors, lawyers, nurses, teachers, and engineers. They work hard. They raise families. They pay taxes. They don't receive public benefits. They are community minded. They are law-abiding. They very rarely commit crimes. When they were growing up in the United States, their parents were all immigrants who instilled in them the American Dream. They make our country better. They call the United States their home. This is the country they have allegiance to.

Another great example of Dreamers integrating into American society and contributing to our society is the fact that there are now Dreamers who serve as police officers. As of July 2026, there are five states that allow DACA recipients to serve as police officers: California, Colorado, Illinois, New Mexico, and Washington. Previously in these states, it was required that a police officer must be a U.S. citizen. However, these states passed laws removing the U.S. citizenship requirement and replacing it with the requirement that police officers must be legally authorized to work in the United States, in addition to meeting all of the other standard police officer qualifications. These states implemented these new laws in order to address police officer shortages and the goal of having a police force that reflects the communities they serve.

However, in 2026, the federal government has made life more difficult for Dreamers and, at the same time, making them more vulnerable to deportation. USCIS has delayed the processing of renewal applications for DACA and accompanying work permits. It's important to note that these are renewal applications, not initial applications. USCIS had already stopped processing new DACA applications July 16, 2021, because of a lawsuit. So, everyone who is applying to renew in 2026 has already been reviewed to see if they qualify, such as documenting when they entered the U.S., at what age, their educational qualifications, and lack of criminal history. For a renewal application, very little needs to be done by the agency, other than fingerprinting and updating their criminal background checks to make sure they haven't committed a felony or serious misdemeanor in the past two years. It's very rare for someone who has already been granted DACA to be denied renewal. This ought to be akin to renewing a driver's license. Unfortunately, due to politics, USCIS has hit the brakes on processing these renewal applications. The effect of this is that thousands of DACA holders have lost their jobs because their work permits have expired. This is not their fault. This is the fault of the U.S. government for delaying the processing of the applications. The federal government has put DACA holders in a vulnerable situation by not renewing their applications in a timely manner. In addition, the Board of Immigration Appeals has recently held that having DACA does not protect someone from deportation, which puts them at further risk of being deported. The federal government should not be squeezing them out of their jobs by delaying their renewals so that their employers have to let them go. This not only hurts them and their families, but it also hurts U.S. employers by forcing them to let go of workers who have DACA, and then having to look for other workers to replace them which may be difficult to do.

In June 2026, there were two police officers with the Los Angeles Police Department whose work permits were not renewed by USCIS in a timely manner, which resulted in these officers being placed on administrative leave and having to turn in their badges and guns because the federal government caused a lapse in their work permits. This was no fault of the officers. This is a case of the federal government not doing its job. There is no good reason that a police department should lose the service of an officer, even temporarily, simply because USCIS has dragged its feet in renewing their work permit.

At a public hearing, Congressman Lou Correa asked DHS Secretary Markwayne Mullin for assistance in having USCIS process DACA renewals in a timely manner, in order for these police officers to be able to continue their employment and service to the community. Secretary Mullin responded, "Absolutely. We'd love to help with this, but as you know, Congressman, the fastest way to actually fix this DACA issue is for Congress to actually pass legislation to fix it." Of course, Congressman Correa has repeatedly advocated for legislation to provide legal status for undocumented people who came to the United States as children.

One of the current legislative proposals that would fix this is The American Dream and Promise Act. This bill would offer Dreamers the ability to apply for conditional lawful permanent residence for 10 years. I would actually propose that Dreamers should have the opportunity to apply for lawful permanent residence that is not conditional for any period of time. These folks are practically Americans as it is because they were brought here as children and they were raised as Americans. As children in school, they literally pledged their allegiance to the United States. For someone who came to the U.S. as a child, under the age of 18, prior to November 3, 2020, it should be enough for them to be people of good moral character who make an application and go through a background check, so that they can live in the United States permanently and eventually apply to become U.S. citizens.

CHAPTER 4

The Biden Years

Where Do We Draw the Line?

WHEN PRESIDENT BIDEN WAS ELECTED on November 3, 2020, there was overwhelming support among Americans to have some sort of legalization or amnesty for the millions of undocumented immigrants who had come to the U.S. many years prior and were settled here, albeit without legal status. The mood quickly changed, though, when millions of people poured into the United States during President Biden's administration. The Border Patrol reported approximately 1.66 million encounters during fiscal year 2021 (beginning October 1, 2020, to September 30, 2021). For fiscal year 2022, that number rose to 2.21 million. It was almost the same in FY2023, at 2.05 million. Then for fiscal year 2024, there were approximately 1.53 million Border Patrol encounters. We, as a nation, were not prepared to properly deal with all of those people coming to our border and asking for help. Although the immigration law provides for mandatory detention of applicants for admission at the border, it was not physically possible for DHS to hold all of those migrants in detention because the numbers were just too large and DHS did not have the detention space to hold all those people. The result is that most of them were allowed to enter the country through various legal mechanisms. Many were just "released on recognizance" after being arrested by the Border Patrol. Others were given "parole." Then, in 2023, DHS under the Biden Administration set up the CBP One app for people to make appointments to enter the U.S. through a legal process. The Department of Homeland Security was overwhelmed because Congress had not, and still has not, prepared for a large influx of asylum seekers at the southern border.

The scenes on television of all of these people coming to the border at once was startling for the American public. For many Americans, there was a sense that these were people in need, and they didn't have a problem with that. But many other Americans felt that our country was being overrun by foreigners who took advantage of our kindness, taking advantage of our asylum laws. Many Americans feel like our country was coerced into letting these people come into the United States, and it wasn't what they wanted. They might feel like these folks barged in and President Biden didn't stop them.

For the millions of people who crossed the border without inspection and then requested asylum, they are now legal asylum seekers and are asking the U.S. government to hear their cases. They fled their countries to escape violence or persecution. The United States has a humanitarian obligation to hear their asylum applications and treat them humanely. Under our laws and our Constitution, they are entitled to due process.

Let's talk about why so many people tried to come to the U.S. any way that they could. They were fleeing horrible situations in their home countries. For example, many Mexicans were trying to escape the violence that has taken over much of that country. Many Venezuelans were coming to escape persecution and economic devastation under Maduro (whom President Trump removed from office and brought to the United States to face criminal charges). Many Cubans came to the U.S. to escape persecution and economic devastation under their own dictator. Haitians were escaping horrific gang violence, plus widespread and deep-seated government corruption.

Imagine what it would be like to live in such places. We take for granted that the economy in our nation will be relatively good and that we won't go hungry. And we take for granted that our police are not in cahoots with the criminals. Pause and think about what it must have been like to live in Venezuela, where few people had jobs, where extreme inflation made even necessities unaffordable. Imagine that kind of inflation. Imagine what it would be like to live in Haiti, where people were kidnapped for ransom by gangs, where street violence was common. So, if you're a decent person from one of these countries, naturally you will do anything you can to leave and find somewhere you can live in peace. That's all they wanted. They wanted to come to the U.S. and live in peace, like generations of earlier immigrants. So you can't blame them for leaving their countries of origin. It seems unfair to blame people for wanting to leave these places and come to the U.S., breathe free, and have a better life.

There is a saying that, before you criticize someone, you should walk a mile in their shoes. In the case of many of the immigrants who fled their home countries and came to the United States seeking a better life, the saying would be, "Walk 60 miles through the Darién gap." You've doubtless heard of the Darién gap. It is a 60-mile stretch of jungle that separates Colombia from Panama. There are no roads. It is a treacherous trek where the intense heat and humidity make it difficult to remain hydrated. In order to pass through it, a person must stumble through rainforests, mountains, swamps, and rivers, alongside dangerous creatures and organized crime. Anybody who attempts to pass through risks death by either dehydration, drowning, disease, or snakes. The area is home to criminals who prey on people by way of extortion, kidnapping, and sexual violence. It is extraordinarily dangerous. For many migrants in south America, a trip through the Darién gap is the only way to get to the United States. Also, many migrants from around the rest of the world who wish to come to the U.S. also pass through the Darién gap because they are not able to travel from their home countries directly to Mexico or central America, so they fly to south America and attempt to make the trip through the Darién gap in hopes of eventually reaching the U.S.

From 2010 to 2020, 115,758 people crossed the Darién gap over the course of a ten-year period. But starting in 2021, there was an enormous increase, caused by people fleeing severe economic and political situations in their home countries. In 2021, 133,653 migrants made the trek (more than all the people put together in the previous ten years). In 2022, that number almost doubled, to 248,284 migrants. Then, in 2023, there was a record of 520,085 migrants who crossed through. In 2024, there were 302,203 migrants who made the journey. These are the numbers of people who exited the Darién gap on the Panama side during those years. But since no record is kept of how many people start the journey from the Colombia side, no one knows how many lives have been lost.

So what do we do with the millions of people who came during the Biden years? We should treat people humanely. We should be treating all of the people who crossed the southern border from 2021–2024 with decency and respect. Even if we're not going to include them in the new Registry group, we should recognize that they have been unjustly vilified. For the most part, they are ordinary people who were faced with extraordinary struggles in their countries due to violence, decimated economies, corrupt police, and governments run by dictators.

Ultimately, whether they stay in the U.S. should depend on their individual asylum applications and if they qualify for any other provision in the law. It's important to hear their asylum claims and make fair, expeditious decisions. But during the process of deciding their fate, our government should, at the very least, not mistreat them. Unfortunately, since January 20, 2025, the federal government has violated their Constitutional rights in many cases. They have been summarily arrested while they attempt to process their asylum applications and then held in horrible conditions of immigration detention centers without bail. With regard to their asylum applications, in many cases the immigration judges have refused to hear their testimony and deported them to third countries.

In order to resolve this crisis humanely and efficiently, and to rectify due process violations, we should immediately release all of these folks who have been summarily arrested by ICE at immigration court and at their check-ins and interviews. Then, we should make room on the Immigration Court docket to hear all of their cases.

CHAPTER 5

Border Security & New Rules for Asylum

EVERYBODY IS SAYING THAT PRESIDENT Trump has secured the border. But there are just a couple things that maybe we could improve on. First, we need to stop the flow of illegal drugs into the United States. And second, we need to have a humane and efficient way for people to request asylum in the United States.

X-Ray Vision on the Border

In June 2026, U.S. Customs and Border Protection (CBP) announced that they had seized more than 1,600 pounds of marijuana in a truckload of chocolate at the Port of Entry to the U.S. at Buffalo, New York. CBP agents discovered sealed plastic bags of marijuana that had been hidden inside cardboard containers of chocolate.

According to reports, the CBP officers who made this discovery just had a hunch about the driver, and sent the truck to secondary inspection where they scanned the cargo with a giant scanner. The federal government refers to this scanning technology as nonintrusive inspection (NII). After an officer scans the cargo, they use advanced technology to detect things that are being concealed.

The CBP press release says, "CBP officers regularly utilize advanced screening technologies, including nonintrusive inspection systems and X-ray imaging, to detect concealed contraband in commercial shipments. These tools, combined with officer expertise and intelligence-driven targeting, are critical to identifying and intercepting illegal narcotics and other prohibited items."

But with this kind of technology available, it raises other questions. Why are there still some drugs being smuggled into the United States? How much of the car and truck traffic into the U.S. is being scanned? Can the drugs be stopped?

On January 5, 2021, President Trump signed a law known as the "Securing America's Ports Act." Under this law, the Department of Homeland Security and its agency Customs and Border Protection (CBP) were required to submit a plan for reaching 100 percent scanning of all commercial vehicles, passenger vehicles, and freight rail traffic coming into the U.S. at land Ports of Entry and rail-border crossings, within 6 years (which will be January 5, 2027). Importantly, though, the law does not actually require the achievement of 100 percent scanning; the law just required a plan.

In January 2022, CBP submitted its scanning plan to Congress. In September 2025, the Government Accountability Office reported that the plan did not include nonintrusive inspection systems needed for nine Ports of Entry on the southwest border, including the two busiest Ports, San Ysidro and Otay Mesa, both near San Diego. CBP officials said that they did not include the nine Ports of Entry because there is not enough physical space to install the systems in the preprimary inspection areas of those Ports (meaning before a vehicle reaches the CBP officer in the booth). The GAO also reported that those nine Ports of Entry, combined together, make up nearly 40 percent of the vehicle traffic on the southern border. So, it's not really a 100 percent plan. It's a plan for the northern border and a little more than half the traffic at the southern border. And even at that, it's unclear when that part of it will be done.

We need to secure Ports of Entry by scanning all the cargo crossing into the United States. As it stands right now, there are gaps. And some of the Ports of Entry that do not have cargo scanning are the largest and busiest border crossing points, such as near San Diego. We need a plan to actually achieve 100 percent scanning. We cannot let this continue to be a perpetual aspiration that never comes to fruition.

That's the only way we're going to effectively reduce drugs coming into the U.S. This requires adding more CBP officers, of course. But most importantly, we need to pass a law that ensures that we have scanning technology at every Port of Entry to scan 100 percent of cargo. CBP's 2022 plan (for 100% minus nine Ports of Entry) specifies 153 large-scale drive-through non-intrusive inspection systems. But as of February 2025, there were only 52 systems fully operational. They're making progress. But it does seem that the goal is elusive.

In 2025, The One Big Beautiful Bill Act (OBBBA) appropriated $6.168 billion for "border security, technology, and screening." It says the money can be used for the "procurement and integration of new non-intrusive inspection equipment and associated civil works." But that money covers other things, too, such as artificial intelligence, upgrading air and sea equipment, and border surveillance technology. So, although there was a lot of money in OBBBA for border security, it doesn't quite get the job done on cargo screening, which is essential to eliminate the flow of drugs into the U.S. In June 2026, The Secure America Act appropriated nearly $70 billion for border security. Of that, $3.45 billion is earmarked for "Border Security, Technology, and Screening," which sounds good, but some of that money will be used for things other than nonintrusive inspection systems. And there's still not a public plan for how to conduct scanning at San Ysidro and Otay Mesa.

This is no doubt a complex problem of how to install scanning technology at these busy Ports with logistical difficulties. But it's hard to believe that, in this day and age, the United States can't figure it out. The Dignity Act also tries to address this issue, as well. It has a border security section and it would authorize $2 billion per year for 10 years to fund the infrastructure, including things like expanding inspection lanes, at land Ports of Entry. That's $20 billion overall to stop the flow of illegal drugs, which could be funded by the restitution fines paid by the currently undocumented immigrants.

When Congress passes common sense immigration reform, it should include the money to achieve true 100 percent NII screening, with all of the associated costs, and it should also include a framework to measure the progress and accountability of CBP. This will help us achieve true border security.

Orderly Processing & Human Rights

No one wants open borders. No one wants for people to be able to cross the border illegally without inspection by an immigration officer. The goal should be this: to physically prevent illegal border crossings, and also to have a system which encourages asylum seekers to avail themselves of a legal and orderly process to enter the U.S., instead of trying to cross illegally.

We need to be prepared to do something more than simply repel people from attempting to enter our country. We need to construct an immigration system that will humanely process them as applicants to enter the United States. We need a process that works. We don't just need to "pause asylum cases." We need to make the process smooth and efficient and make sure it has integrity and treats people with dignity. This would involve a physical location for the government (Border Patrol officers, asylum officers, and immigration judges) to hear their asylum applications and decide whether or not to let them into the United States. This was the concept of Ellis Island: A place for immigrants to come to where there's a process to either let them in or not let them in. But we don't really have anything like this anymore.

The Dignity Act would establish three Humanitarian Campuses along the U.S. border with Mexico. Under the Dignity Act, if someone came to the border and requested asylum, as many people did during 2021–2024, they would be held in these facilities. They would be "locked facilities" in the sense that people are not released into the United States, but the facilities don't have to feel like jail. And someone who comes to the U.S. to request asylum certainly shouldn't be treated as a criminal. In fact, by coming to a Port-of-Entry and asking for asylum, that's "doing it the right way." It would be a place where people are treated humanely, with dignity and respect. The Dignity Act would change the asylum process so that everyone who applies for asylum would receive a decision within 60 days. If asylum is granted, then they would be allowed to enter the United States and have legal status. If they are denied, they would be deported. The Dignity Act would provide important improvements to have an orderly, lawful process for asylum seekers.

I would suggest just a few modifications to the Dignity Act's provisions regarding reforming the asylum process.

First, in order to process each asylum application more efficiently, the government should provide legal representation to the asylum applicants. Having an attorney to help fill out their applications and organize their documents would ensure that it's a fair process. Asylum law is extremely complicated and it's not fair to expect an asylum applicant to navigate that process alone.

Second, the timeline of 60 days should be reconsidered. With all that goes into an asylum application, and then also considering that the application and documents will need to be submitted at least a couple weeks before the final interview, I believe a better timeline would be to have the case completed within 90 days, instead of 60.

Third, The Dignity Act requires two asylum officers to decide each case, and would require agreement between the two of them to either grant or deny. The Dignity Act also has a provision for referral to an immigration judge if the two asylum officers cannot agree, or if they think it's a very complicated case that should be decided by a judge. And under the Dignity Act, if someone's case is referred to an immigration judge, then the person is released into the United States to attend court wherever they decide to live. I submit that it would actually work better if we have the immigration judges go to them and hear their testimony at the Humanitarian Campus, instead of the applicants going to the immigration court in some other city, such as Los Angeles or Chicago. Technically, a judge could do it by video but, in evaluating a life-or-death decision such as this, there's no substitute for the judge sitting next to the applicant in the courtroom to evaluate their claim. Also, from a border security standpoint, it would be better to have immigration judges decide an applicant's fate while they're at the Humanitarian Campus, because if the asylum seeker must leave in the event that their case is denied, we shouldn't let them establish a life here and *then* ask them to leave. Understandably, once someone has established a life in the United States, nobody wants to leave.

Physical border security goes hand in hand with providing asylum seekers an orderly way to come to the U.S. and ask for protection. Orderly processing of asylum applications would actually make the job of Border Patrol so much easier because people would have a legal mechanism to request asylum that did not involve just crossing illegally. If we do this, then we'll have a designated place and process for people to come to the U.S. and ask for asylum. This would be a dramatic improvement over what we have now, which is that we can only either hold asylum seekers in immigration jail or release them into the U.S. for protracted deportation proceedings. Neither of those are great options, and the Dignity Act has a reasonable solution.

Asylum

As of mid-2026, there were approximately 1.5 million asylum applications that are pending with USCIS waiting for a decision. Many of these people have now been waiting years for decisions because the system is so backed up. These are folks who are living and working in the United States who tried to "do it the right way." They are waiting for our government to make a decision on their applications. The problem is not "vetting." The problem is that there is just a gigantic number of backlogged applications, partly due to so many applying that it has overwhelmed the system, and partly due to USCIS having policies that lead to long wait times for decisions.

A "pause" in such decisions, as some would have you believe is the right thing to do, is nothing more than throwing up our hands and doing nothing. For the most part, in 2026, many people have already stopped coming to the U.S. for asylum. The current administration has already severely limited the number of immigrants entering the U.S. in one way or another. The question, then, is what are we going to do about all of those people waiting for a decision?

When my father was an immigration officer with INS in the 1970s, he said the best advice he ever got from a supervisor was to "look for reasons to approve the case," instead of "looking for reasons to deny" the case. This is a question of culture within the organization. Nowadays, an asylum officer might spend half a day or more interviewing an applicant. Then, they write up a report and submit it to a supervisor. I have seen cases where people are then re-interviewed one or two more times, and then still have to wait longer for a decision. The way to get through a 1.5 million case backlog is to give USCIS officers the power to approve cases that are clearly approvable and cut down on the bureaucracy. I'm suggesting that USCIS be given the green light to work through them efficiently, without undue delay, and give answers to both the applicants and the American people about whether these folks can stay.

By the way, as for the question of "vetting," remember, these are folks who have now lived among us for years waiting for decisions on their applications. You might say that we have already *de facto* vetted them by letting them live here and the fact that by and large they have demonstrated they are law-abiding good people.

These are folks who came to the U.S. and are afraid to go back to their home countries, for one reason or another. Asylum law is complicated. To qualify for asylum, a person must show that it is more likely than not that they would be persecuted in their home country based on their race, religion, nationality, political opinion, or "membership in a particular social group."

The asylum applicants are victims. They are testifying that their government did some horrible things or let some other bad people in their country get away with doing horrible things. These asylum applicants are from places like Cuba and Venezuela, where people have suffered under dictatorships. Our government even went so far as to invade Venezuela, arrest its dictator, and "take over" the country. So, if our government believes that Maduro was so bad, we shouldn't be too skeptical when we hear the stories of asylum seekers.

Unfortunately, after 2025 there is now a process known as "pretermitting asylum applications," because the U.S. government has made an agreement with an alternative country where the immigrant is not from, and then the U.S. deports the person to that third country. The United States government pays these third countries to take asylum-seekers who are here trying to go through the lawful process. You should know that the government is disqualifying asylum applicants before they even hear their story, just because the government wants to get rid of people as fast as they can. We need our government to stop doing this to people. In our new system, we should end this practice of stopping the immigration judges from hearing the testimony of the asylum applicants.

Let's remember who we are. We are the United States of America, and we can treat people with dignity and respect. We need to take the time to hear what happened to them in their country and why they left.

One final note about asylum. There are many immigrants who have been granted something called "withholding of removal" which is similar to asylum, in that an immigration judge has ruled that a person would be persecuted in their home country, and withholding of removal protects the person from being deported back to that country. In other words, they won their case in court to be protected from deportation to their home country because their life is in danger there. A grant of withholding of removal does not allow the person to apply for a green card. It just protects them from being deported to their home country where they would probably be killed. Under the current administration, there is a new practice where the government now deports these people to a third country that the U.S. has paid to take them. But we're not sending them to the best places. In many cases, we're sending them to dangerous countries or countries who turn around and deport them back to their original countries where we've already decided their life would be in danger. This cruel practice needs to end, and we should eliminate it when we reform the immigration laws.

CHAPTER 6

Make Immigration Court Constitutional

THE IMMIGRATION COURT IS WHERE immigration judges decide who stays and who goes. Does the immigrant get to live in the United States, or does the immigrant have to depart the U.S. and go somewhere else? This decision is the job of an immigration judge. Immigration judges are the people who watch over the process of deporting someone. It's their job to make sure the process is fair. Immigration judges make several types of decisions that profoundly affect people's lives. They decide, for instance, if a person will continue to be present in the U.S. with their spouse and children. That same decision may result in the whole family leaving the United States and moving to another country, and it's uncertain what their life will be like there. If the person is applying for asylum because they believe their life would be threatened in their home country, the immigration judge is making a possibly life-or-death decision for this person. Also, when ICE arrests someone, it has historically been the immigration judge's job to decide if the person should be able to pay a bond and get out on bail. With such serious consequences hanging in the balance, it's vitally important to make sure the immigration judges are neutral, fair adjudicators who are not influenced by whoever is in the White House.

When people think about courts in the United States, people think of independence. A judge is supposed to be impartial. He or she is not supposed to favor either side. It should go without saying that the judge will make up his or her own mind on what to do. And the judge isn't supposed to be thinking about whether or not he or she will be fired because of ruling for one side or the other.

Prior to 2025, immigration judges had a reputation for being fair and impartial when they heard cases to decide whether an immigrant should be allowed to stay in the U.S., or must depart.

When immigrants made applications in immigration court to stay here, immigration judges made sometimes difficult decisions about which cases to grant and which cases to deny. I saw that immigration judges took their jobs seriously as fact finders to discern the truth and apply the law fairly. Immigration judges showed compassion for asylum seekers who had been persecuted in their home countries, and they carefully scrutinized immigrants' testimony about things that had happened to them in their home countries. For immigrants who had lived in the U.S. many years without status and had U.S.-born children, these judges often struggled with the decision of which cases rose to the level of "exceptional and extremely unusual hardship" required to be shown by the immigrant to merit a grant of Cancellation of Removal. In cases of lawful permanent residents who had committed criminal offenses that made them deportable from the U.S., immigration judges tried to have the wisdom to know if a particular immigrant was truly rehabilitated and deserved a second chance to stay in the country with their family. I have seen some judges with extraordinary wisdom and compassion, who understand the impact that their decisions will have on the life of the immigrant before them and their family, and also the community at large.

If an immigrant was arrested and detained for possible deportation, there was a legal process for them to apply for a bond (bail) to be released from immigration custody. The immigration judge would conduct a short hearing, usually 10-15 minutes, where the judge determined if the person might be a danger to the community or a flight risk who might not appear for future court hearings. If the person had lived in the U.S. for many years, had kids who were U.S. citizens, and did not have any criminal history, the judge would routinely set a bond amount for the person to pay to get out custody so they could live with their family while they attended immigration court hearings. Or, if a noncitizen had recently been convicted of a serious crime, the immigration judge would deny bond for "danger."

There are currently approximately 700 immigration judges in the United States. In Immigration Court, immigration judges are employees of the Department of Justice and the prosecuting attorneys work for the Department of Homeland Security. And both of those agencies work for the President of the United States. So, it has always been the case that the judge and the prosecutor ultimately worked for the same boss, the President. Nonetheless, prior to 2025, even though the Immigration Court was not truly independent, there was not a sense that the system was inherently unfair.

Prior to 2025, it was rare for an immigration judge to be fired. It used to be that practically nobody ever got fired. The only way an immigration judge would ever get fired was for misconduct, which rarely happened. The approximately 700 immigration judges were free to apply the law to individual cases as they saw fit, and judges managed their dockets with goals of both completing cases efficiently and also ensuring due process. Each immigration judge has a record of how many asylum cases are granted or denied. But the judge's grant rate did not affect his or her employment, one way or the other.

Then came the purge. Several things have happened with the Immigration Court since January 2025, which have highlighted the lack of independence of the immigration judges and exemplified how the Immigration Court has become an extension of the administration's immigration policy. First, and most notably, the current administration has fired immigration judges who were perceived by the administration to not align with the administration's goals of mass deportations. Second, the administration announced a new mandatory detention policy of detaining immigrants without bond who would have previously qualified to be released on bond while their deportation/removal court proceedings were pending, and the administration has leaned on the immigration judges to carry out this policy even though federal judges have found that it is unlawful.

Starting in January 2025, the current administration fired judges who were perceived to not be aggressive enough in deporting people. In the days following January 20, 2025, the Department of Justice fired 4 senior immigration judges, including the Chief Immigration Judge. In February 2025, the Department of Justice fired approximately 20 more judges, including 5 assistant chief immigration judges and 15 new immigration judges who had been hired by the previous administration, had gone through judge training, and were scheduled to be sworn in. In April 2025, the DOJ fired at least 8 more immigration judges.

At the time, there were almost 4 million pending deportation cases, including approximately 1.5 million asylum cases. On April 21, 2025, the President posted the following statement on social media which may have revealed the administration's intentions: "We cannot give everyone a trial, because to do so would take, without exaggeration, 200 years. We would need hundreds of thousands of trials for the hundreds of thousands of illegals we are sending out of the Country. Such a thing is not possible to do." Regrettably, it seems that the administration's answer to how to work through such a huge backlog of cases was to simply go fast and sometimes deny the case without even letting the immigrant tell their story. And to accomplish this goal, they would need to get rid of immigration judges who believed part of the job description was to give everyone their day in court and decide cases fairly (in other words, abide by due process under the Constitution).

On July 3, 2025, the DOJ fired an assistant chief judge in Chicago with a three sentence termination email while she was on vacation, without any explanation.

Also in early December 2025, the DOJ fired a U.S. Army Reserve lawyer that the administration had detailed to be a temporary immigration judge. Since the start of his detail as a temporary immigration judge, he had granted 6 of the 11 deportation cases he presided over in November. Some have surmised that the reason for his termination is that he granted too many cases.

In 2025, the San Francisco Immigration Court started with 21 immigration judges. By November 2025, 12 of them had been fired, leaving just 9 immigration judges. These judges had a record of granting a lot of asylum cases. By January 2026, only 4 immigration judges remained in the San Francisco Immigration Court. The DOJ then announced that the San Francisco Immigration Court would close and all of the cases would be transferred to other courts.

In total, the Department of Justice has fired over 100 immigration judges since January 20, 2025. They fired judges who were respected for their professionalism, integrity, and expertise in immigration law. These were judges who did their jobs with as much judicial independence as they could. But judicial independence is not valued by an administration whose chief aim is to deport as many people as possible, as fast as possible.

In November 2025, the Department of Justice advertised for new immigration judges across the country to replace judges who have been fired. The announcement read, "Apply today to become a deportation judge." The job advertisement went on to say, "Make decisions with generational consequences. Ensure that only aliens with legally meritorious claims are allowed to remain." What do you think that means? There certainly can be profound generational consequences when a person gets deported. If a man has been living in the U.S. for 25 years, has raised kids here, and is continuing to raise kids here, kids who are U.S. citizens, then yes, it will have generational consequences on his family if his kids either have to live without their parent, or for his kids to have to leave the U.S. to go live with that parent in another country. Why not aspire to make decisions that will "Ensure that *all* aliens with legally meritorious claims are allowed to remain"?

What happened to immigration bail?

When Congress passed the current immigration laws in 1996, the Immigration Court (formally known as Executive Office for Immigration Review) and INS (what we used to call "Immigration") both got together and wrote regulations to implement the law. The regulations were published in the Federal Register on March 6, 1997, and the regulations said that if an undocumented noncitizen who had crossed the border illegally was arrested by immigration authorities inside the United States (not at or near the border), an immigration judge could let them out on bail if they were not a danger or a flight risk. So, if a noncitizen was arrested by immigration authorities in Los Angeles, Phoenix, or anywhere else in the interior of the U.S., an immigration judge could allow them to post a bond and get released from immigration custody while they attended their Immigration Court hearings. The regulations were kind of like the owner's manual on how the law that Congress had passed would work. And up until July 8, 2025, everybody knew that's what the law was. In fact, if you had an immigration court bond hearing on July 7, 2025, the prosecutor and the judge both knew that this was the law, and that if the person the government was trying to deport had come to the U.S. illegally, then the judge could decide whether or not the person was a danger or flight risk, and decide whether or not they should get a bond. Prior to July 8, 2025, all the immigration judges and prosecutors knew that if a noncitizen had entered the U.S. several years ago without permission and had been living here since that time, then if they got caught by ICE, they would be eligible for bail. But on that day, July 8, 2025, the Acting ICE Director put out a memo saying that all undocumented noncitizens present in the United States who had entered the U.S. without inspection could not be released from custody on bond, from that day forward.

The memo came from ICE, but the immigration judges aren't part of ICE. ICE is an agency of the Department of Homeland Security. The judges, though, are part of the Department of Justice. But as soon as the ICE memo came out on July 8, 2025, DHS attorneys started arguing to the immigration judges that, even though they both knew yesterday on July 7 that the law was that a non-citizen who entered illegally was eligible for bond under the law, that starting July 8, the new interpretation would be that none of the millions of people in the U.S. who crossed the border without documentation would be eligible to be released on bond if they got arrested by ICE. That was ICE's new rule on July 8, 2025. This was not a new law passed by Congress. This was the Acting ICE Director coming out with a new, novel interpretation of the law that flew in the face of what everyone had understood the law to be for almost 30 years. According to the ICE memo, after July 8,

2025, immigration judges no longer had discretion to release undocumented immigrants from detention centers by posting bond.

Many of the immigrants who were locked up appealed. In immigration, a person appeals the decision of the immigration judge to the Board of Immigration Appeals (also a part of the Department of Justice). Then, in September 2025, the Board of Immigration Appeals quickly decided a case called *Matter of Yajure-Hurtado* where the Board agreed with DHS that this new interpretation of the law had actually been the law the whole time, since 1996, and it was the "plain language" of the statute. It was simply a mistake, they said, that the government had done the opposite for decades.

Well, if it was the "plain language" of the statute, and if it was as clear as day, like they said, why did the immigration court and INS interpret it the exact opposite when they published the regulations in 1997, to allow for people to be released on bond? If it was so obvious, why had the judges and government attorneys agreed for almost 30 years that a person who came to the U.S. without a visa years ago and lived in this country, *could* get a bond?

Since the change on July 8, 2025, many federal district court judges have ruled that the government is breaking the law by doing this because Section 236(a) of the Immigration and Nationality Act says a person who has been living in the United States *can* be released on bond if they're not a danger or a flight risk. Federal judges have also ruled that this practice of mandatory detention is a violation of Due Process under the Fifth Amendment of the U.S. Constitution, which says the government cannot take away a person's freedom (liberty) and lock them up without following fair procedures and the law. However, immigration judges have been threatened with disciplinary action if they follow the federal judges' interpretation of the law instead of the government's interpretation. This puts the immigration judges in the position of possibly being disciplined or fired if they follow the law as declared by a federal judge.

As of this writing, four Circuit Courts of Appeal have ruled that DHS's new interpretation is unlawful, and there are two Circuit Courts of Appeal that have gone along with the administration's new interpretation of the law. This has created a "circuit split" where different courts have reached different conclusions about the same issue. Because of the circuit split, the Supreme Court will hear a case on this issue and rule on it sometime after the publication of this book.

It is possible that the Supreme Court will rule in favor of the government's new interpretation of the law, and let the government keep noncitizens locked up without bail. But either way, what has become clear is that the immigration court is not independent. The court administration has pressured immigration judges to follow the administration's interpretation of the law regarding bond eligibility, and told the immigration judges not to follow what the federal court judges say the law is. If the immigration judges were independent, they would not worry about getting fired for following a federal court judge's order.

Article I of the U.S. Constitution

The cure for this is to make immigration court independent. The way to do that is to take the immigration court out of the Department of Justice and make it an Article I court, that is authorized as a court under the U.S. Constitution, like the Tax court or the Bankruptcy court.

A lot of knowledgeable immigration people have advocated that Immigration Court should be an "Article I" court, instead of being a branch of the Department of Justice. Article I of the U.S. Constitution gives Congress the power to create special courts under the Supreme Court, to rule on how federal laws should be applied. These courts are independent of any agency in the federal government. Congress could do the same thing with Immigration Court.

Congress could take Immigration Court out of the Department of Justice and make it independent, to operate in a neutral way authorized by the Constitution and with Congressional oversight.

Doing this would mean that immigration judges would be a "check" on ICE, so that ICE can't just do whatever it wants without being checked. The problem right now is that the Executive branch (DHS and DOJ) controls both the prosecution and the courtroom. And who controls the Executive branch? The President. The President controls the immigration courts because the judges work for the Attorney General in the Department of Justice, and the Attorney General works for the President. This gives the President tremendous power over who gets deported. Immigration judges know who they work for. So they have to be very careful to not make decisions that people higher up in the administration would disagree with, or to appear too "pro immigrant." They have one eye on the case, and one eye on their job.

If Congress passed a law that made Immigration Court an Article I court, independent of the Department of Homeland Security and Department of Justice, the judges could act like real judges who are impartial decision makers.

If you take the Immigration Court out of the Department of Justice, then an immigration judge wouldn't have to worry about being fired if they grant too many cases or if they let a noncriminal undocumented immigrant out on bail. By having an independent Article I Immigration Court, the Attorney General or Acting ICE Director can't dictate the outcomes of large groups of cases simply by writing a memo with a new interpretation of the law. The very act of Congress making Immigration Court an Article I court would be a check on the Executive branch, making the Executive branch a little less all-powerful in immigration enforcement. This would ensure the integrity of the Immigration Court.

There is currently a bill in Congress called the Real Courts, Rule of Law Act. Under this bill, Immigration Court would be made a Constitutional court under Article I of the U.S. Constitution. If Congress passed a law that made Immigration Court an Article I court, independent of the Department of Homeland Security and Department of Justice, the judges could act as impartial decision-makers whose jobs don't depend on which side wins: the usual role of a judge. This would accomplish the goal of making immigration court independent. One reason that all Americans should support this is the idea of separation of powers. With an independent immigration court, the Executive branch could still enforce the immigration law but would not also control the referees. Therefore, I would propose that the Real Courts, Rule of Law Act should be part of common sense immigration reform.

Jurisdiction and Discretion

Immigration judges should have more power to decide cases. In lawyer language, this is called "jurisdiction." If someone has jurisdiction, this means "whether something is in their power." You'd be surprised how much this is an issue in immigration court. Oftentimes, there's a crucial issue in someone's case that needs to be decided by U.S. Citizenship and Immigration Services (USCIS) (an agency of the Department of Homeland Security). But under the current immigration laws an immigration judge does not have the power to fix it. This is because a different government agency has jurisdiction over some important part of the case, and the judge can't decide that part of the case. For example, suppose that an immigrant's spouse or adult U.S. citizen son or daughter files a petition with USCIS for the immigrant to become a lawful permanent resident. After the petition is approved by USCIS, the immigration judge can grant the immigrant's application for lawful permanent residence. But it sometimes takes a year or more for USCIS to adjudicate this kind of petition, which doesn't involve much more than proving the relationship. It's frankly ridiculous that it takes them so long. And the immigration judge can't decide the case until USCIS has made its decision on the petition. This causes a huge waste of time and money for the government because the judge has to keep continuing the case waiting on USCIS to do something, or there is pressure on the judge to finish the case without waiting for USCIS to make a decision (resulting in the person being ordered to leave).

We can make this more efficient by just letting the immigration judge decide everything that needs to be decided, even if it could also be done by USCIS but they just haven't gotten around to it yet.

This is especially a problem because there are some types of cases, such as U visas for crime victims who provide aid to law enforcement, that have backlogs of up to five years. And if ICE steps in and says they want to deport the person, then even though they qualify for the U visa, the person has to go to immigration court. Under the current law, the immigration judge doesn't have jurisdiction over the U visa to approve it and give it to the immigrant. We could make the government more efficient by giving immigration judges the power to grant U visas. (To facilitate this, we also need to eliminate the cap on the number of U visas that are allowed to be granted each year, to eliminate the backlog of cases that have been provisionally approved but are just waiting for a visa number to be available.) This would give the immigration judge the power to adjudicate everything in a case, and not have to wait for somebody else in the government to do it. Give the judge jurisdiction over any application that a person is eligible for, and the government will be more efficient.

Another issue in Immigration Court is that the current immigration law severely limits which cases and how many a judge can grant. One way to give immigration judges more discretion is to roll back one of the harshest sections of the 1996 IIRIRA, called "Cancellation of Removal." Prior to 1996, an immigration judge could grant a non-criminal immigrant a pardon called "Suspension of Deportation" if the person had lived in the United States for more than 7 years and had an immediate family member who was a U.S. citizen or permanent resident. Under the Suspension of Deportation law, immigration judges had broad discretion to grant cases for deserving undocumented immigrants who qualified. But in 1996, Congress eliminated Suspension of Deportation and replaced it with Cancellation of Removal, which is now the law. For someone to qualify for the current Cancellation of Removal for non-permanent residents, that person has to prove a number of things. First, they have to show that they've lived in the United States for at least 10 years, instead of 7. Then, they have to have a "qualifying relative," meaning a spouse, child, or parent who is a U.S. citizen or permanent resident. Then, the law says that to win, they have to show that the hardship to their particular spouse, parent, or child will be "exceptionally and extremely unusual hardship" if the noncitizen is deported. This is a very high bar, unreachable for most people. Most people won't qualify because, even if they've lived in the U.S. for a long time and their kids are U.S. citizens, if the relatives don't have any serious health, medical, educational, or psychological issues, then the judge will say the hardship to those relatives is "ordinary," "that which is to be expected of family separation."

The law severely limits the number of people who can win this type of case. There is an annual limit of 4,000 cases that immigration judges can grant each year. Out of the millions of undocumented immigrants in the United States, there are only a precious few 4,000 Cancellation of Removal applications that can be granted each year.

A sensible, common-sense change would be to go back to the old rule of "Suspension of Deportation" and give immigration judges discretion again to grant noncitizens' applications to stay here with their families, instead of the current restrictive law of "Cancellation of Removal" which essentially ties the judges' hands so they can't grant most cases. And we should eliminate the cap on the number of cases that can be approved.

CHAPTER 7

Temporary Protected Status

AS MANY AMERICANS KNOW BY now, TPS stands for Temporary Protected Status. TPS was enacted under the Immigration Act of 1990 after much Senate debate over America's moral obligation to give safe haven in a world where people are endangered by civil war or epidemics or natural disasters in their home countries, versus the reality that countries do not return to safety overnight and there was an anxiety in Congress that what is intended to be a temporary safe haven oftentimes becomes permanent.

In fact, the main opponent of TPS at the time was Senator Alan Simpson, a Republican from Wyoming, who prophesied that it would lead to people staying permanently. He said, "There is nothing so permanent in U.S. immigration law as a temporary status." He foresaw that if the government granted safe haven to tens of thousands of people from a war-torn country, granting work permits and legal protection from deportation, that those immigrants would naturally set down roots here. That's what people do, once the period of getting settled is over, they build their lives. So, of course, someone with TPS is going to get a job and work hard, pay taxes, hopefully buy a house, and have children. And once they do all that and become part of the community, it's unpopular with

Americans to make them leave. Simpson knew this. He didn't like it, but he agreed to it because it was important to him to pass the rest of the 1990 immigration law to help businesses in the U.S. In other words, it was well-known in Congress when they enacted TPS in 1990 that "temporary" might not mean temporary.

Prior to 2025, there were a total of 29 countries for which the United States had ever granted Temporary Protected Status since 1990. Of those, the United States had terminated 12 of those TPS designations, all as a result of actual changes in the countries which made it somewhat safe for people to return. In those cases, the U.S. terminated the TPS designations and asked those immigrants to return to their home countries. Because the conditions in those countries had stabilized, it was relatively noncontroversial for the most part to terminate those TPS designations. For example, Kuwait was designated for TPS in 1991 and then terminated in 1992 after the end of the Persian Gulf War. Many of the TPS designations were terminated because civil wars ended, in such places as Lebanon, Bosnia-Herzegovina, Guinea-Bissau, and Angola. In other cases, TPS designations were terminated because catastrophes had been resolved, such earthquakes, volcanic eruptions, or Ebola virus epidemics. None of those 12 TPS terminations prior to 2025 were controversial because of politics or racial animus. In fact, the reason that the terminations were noncontroversial is because they happened as a result of real change in those countries, such as the end of wars or epidemics. For the first 11 terminations, the average length of designation was less than 4 years.

But the 12th termination was different. Liberia had been designated for Temporary Protected Status for a staggering 26 years. The U.S. originally granted TPS to citizens of Liberia way back in 1991 and then terminated the designation in 2017 due to the end of civil wars and the Ebola crisis there. By that time, thousands of Liberians had been living in the U.S. for an extraordinary amount of time, far beyond what anyone would say was "temporary." During those years, Liberians made significant contributions to the United States. They earned a well-deserved reputation for being vital healthcare workers as Certified Nursing Assistants, Home Health Aides, and Registered Nurses. When the U.S. terminated the TPS designation for Liberia in 2017, the most vocal advocacy for a solution to their immigration status came from the healthcare industry because of the impending labor shortages they would face without Liberians who had already been essential workers for years. Hospital networks pointed out that many of the Liberian healthcare workers had been working at the same healthcare jobs for more than 10 years, and that it would be devastating for the hospitals to lose them.

So, Congress stepped in and fixed the problem. The Liberian Refugee Immigration Fairness Act (LRIF) was passed as part of the National Defense Authorization Act for Fiscal Year 2020, and signed into law by President Trump on December 20, 2019. LRIF allowed Liberians who had been physically present in the U.S. since at least November 20, 2014, to apply for lawful permanent residence. (They decided on the 2014 cutoff date because that was when West Africa suffered a devastating Ebola outbreak.)

The requirements to apply were that an applicant had to prove they were Liberian and that they had lived in the U.S continuously since the cutoff date. They were disqualified if they had been convicted of an aggravated felony, two or more crimes involving moral turpitude, or had ever persecuted someone. To apply, applicants had to submit significant documentation to show their physical presence in the U.S., pay a $1,225 filing fee, do a criminal background check, and submit a medical examination.

The Liberian Refugee Immigration Fairness Act was not amnesty, but rather a recognition these Liberians had become part of the fabric of our society and our workforce. To uproot these

Liberians would have caused significant damage to healthcare in the United States, so Congress made the decision to let them stay permanently. This law was an acknowledgment by Congress and President Trump that "temporary" doesn't always mean temporary.

As of March 2025, the United States was home to nearly 1.3 million people who had been granted Temporary Protected Status. The individuals came from 17 different countries, but just five countries account for approximately 97% of all the TPS holders as of 2025. These top five countries are Venezuela, Haiti, El Salvador, Ukraine, and Honduras.

Under Section 244 of the INA, DHS has broad power to review and terminate these country-specific designations. But just because our government has terminated a TPS designation doesn't mean that we as a nation should just leave it at that and make those people leave. In fact, I propose that for any TPS country where it's still not safe for people to return, and where there is a good case to be made that those TPS recipients make significant contributions to the United States, we should consider changing the law to invite them to apply for lawful permanent residence just like we did for the Liberians.

Haiti, For Example

The country of Haiti is an incredibly chaotic and dangerous place. Gangs commit murder, extort businesses, traffic drugs and guns, kidnap people, and rape women and girls with impunity. Although some of the rapes are perpetrated by individuals, 81 percent of the sexual violence is gang rape. Police and self-defense groups attempt to combat the gangs, but the gangs have military grade weapons, so this often results in more murder. The evidence is overwhelming that Haiti is not a safe place where Haitian TPS holders can go back home to.

In 2026, there are approximately 350,000 Haitians living in the United States with Temporary Protected Status. For Haitian TPS holders, the average length of time that they have lived in the U.S. is 13 years. 200,000 Haitian TPS holders work to take care of their families and have a reputation for being great workers. Having them as part of the workforce enhances the quality of life for ordinary Americans. There are currently 22,000 Haitians who work as cooks and servers. There is an equal number of Haitians who work as stockers and packers to fulfill our online orders of goods. About 15,000 Haitians do agricultural work. 14,000 Haitians work in retail and customer service. The elderly in the United States are cared for by 8,000 Haitian caregivers. And 7,000 Haitians work in U.S. factories to make American made products

As they work, they pay $800 million per year in federal and payroll taxes, and pay $755 million in state and local taxes.

In June 2026, after the Supreme Court ruled that DHS was allowed to terminate TPS for Haiti, Ohio Governor Mike DeWine went on television and said that it was a mistake to terminate TPS for Haiti. He directly criticized the administration's decision because (1) Haiti is not a safe place due to the ongoing violence, and (2) it's bad for the United States to force them to leave because Haitians have become such an integral part of communities and the workforce.

Haitians share our values. The Catholic Bishops of Ohio and Florida have also spoken up on behalf of Haitian TPS holders, stating, "They are active members of local communities who work, raise families, and participate deeply in religious life." Archbishop Thomas Wenski of Miami vouched for Haitian TPS recipients, stating, "They are hard workers filling jobs that, were it not for them, would go unfilled." Haitian TPS holders are good, hard working people, and we are lucky to have them in the United States. It's truly a shame that they were displaced from their home country.

But the United States has, once again, been the beneficiary of a large group of wonderful immigrants seeking refuge who end up contributing to make America a better place. This is just a small overview of why Haitian TPS holders should be allowed to apply for lawful permanent residence.

Each of the 17 TPS countries has a story. They are all places you wouldn't want to visit right now in 2026 because of extreme danger or economic devastation. These are the same reasons it wouldn't be safe for TPS recipients to return. The people from these countries have been wonderful guests in our country. They have made significant contributions to the United States and have become part of the fabric of our country, similar to the Liberians. We should recognize these things and change the immigration law to keep them here. Although they came here for temporary refuge, they have become deeply woven into our communities and our nation. They share our American values and make America great.

As part of common sense immigration reform, we should pass a new law to give Haitians on TPS the same deal we gave Liberians on TPS. This would be in the best interests of the United States and also be the most humane thing to do. In addition, we should look at each of the other TPS countries to see if there are reasons to treat TPS holders from those countries equally. Many, if not all, will merit equal treatment because those other countries also are still not safe to return to and the TPS holders from those countries make similar substantial contributions to the United States.

CHAPTER 8

Optimize Legal Immigration

Make It Make Sense, Make America Stronger

IMMIGRATION HAS BEEN A DRIVING force in America for over 250 years. It is something special to the United States that has been instrumental in the growth of our great nation. But if we wish to continue on our journey to greatness, we need to continue to welcome immigrants and improve our legal immigration system to make America stronger.

The following pages are an overview of how immigration works in the United States under the current law. This chapter is devoted to the nuts and bolts of immigration law as it applies to people applying for visas and green cards, and how the legal immigration system can be improved to make the United States stronger. This chapter proposes several changes we need to make. One of these is to make it easier for farmers to bring in agricultural workers from other countries and legalize the undocumented farmworkers who are already here in the U.S. growing our food. Second, the United States needs more skilled workers, which requires changes to the current immigration laws to accomplish this. Also, when people talk about immigrants "waiting in line" for visas to become available, people ignore that the waiting times are absurd for both family-based and employment-based immigration. For family-based immigrants, these long wait times defeat the goal of family reunification. For employment-based immigrants, these long wait times deprive U.S. businesses and our society in general from getting the benefit of having the best of the best come to the U.S. In addition, our legal immigration system is riddled with legal landmines that make it impossible or unnecessarily complicated for certain people to immigrate, and these barriers do not serve legitimate purposes. Many of these reforms are currently being proposed in various bills, such as the Farm Workforce Modernization Act, the Dignity Act, and the Essential Workers for Economic Advancement Act.

How to Get a Visa

In order to enter the United States legally with a visa, you have to qualify for one of those visas. What you're coming to the U.S. to do has to fit one of the visa categories, and you have to meet all the requirements for that visa. First, there are nonimmigrant visas, which are for a temporary stay in the United States for a specific purpose, such as visiting, going to school, working on a temporary basis, and so on. Nonimmigrant visas are specifically for things that are supposed to be limited to a temporary time period, and then you're supposed to go home when it's over. Second, there are immigrant visas, which are for permanent residence in the United States. Being admitted on an immigrant visa is called being admitted as a Lawful Permanent Resident. (For someone already legally in the United States, this can also sometimes be accomplished through a process called Adjustment of Status which does not require leaving the U.S.) Immigrant visas are mainly for either family members of U.S. citizens or lawful permanent residents, or very valuable workers, or lucky people who win the diversity lottery, along with a handful of other less common pathways.

Nonimmigrant visas

There are many types of nonimmigrant visas for people coming to the U.S. temporarily to do such things as visit, work, or study. Nonimmigrant visas are identified by letters of the alphabet, such as B for visitor, F for student, and K for fiancée. There are different visas for different employment categories, such as A visas for diplomats, E visas for investors, and H-1B visas for professionals. Other interesting visas are O visas for artists and entertainers and P visas for professional athletes. But you will notice that there is not a visa for construction workers, caregivers, or restaurant workers. So if a person wanted to come to the United States legally for the purpose of working in one of these industries, it has not been possible... because there's not a nonimmigrant visa available for them under the current immigration laws. A solution for this would be the Essential Workers for Economic Advancement Act, discussed below. For farm workers, there is a category called the H2A visa but the H2A visa program doesn't meet all the U.S. need for agricultural workers. This could be fixed by the Farm Workforce Modernization Act which is a bill that has been introduced in Congress.

Amber Waves of Grain

Back around 1990, there were about 14 percent of crop farmworkers who were undocumented. At that time, there were approximately 443,000 crop farmworkers, so 14 percent equaled 62,000 undocumented crop farmworkers in 1990.

Those numbers have grown tremendously. As of 2025, there were approximately 1 million crop farmworkers in the U.S. (more than double the number in 1990). The number of undocumented crop farmworkers exploded to 40%. That's approximately 400,000 undocumented crop farmworkers in 2025, working to grow our food.

In addition, there are approximately 200,000 additional undocumented workers who work in other agricultural jobs besides crop farming.

That's approximately 600,000 undocumented workers actively working to grow the food we eat. Of course we want them to continue to live and work in the United States so we can continue to enjoy the standard of living to which we have become accustomed.

The current H2A visa program has not helped this problem because of its restrictive rules that make it unworkable for the employers. For example, the H2A visa is only for seasonal jobs, not for year-round work. Also, jobs in certain industries do not qualify, such as the livestock, hog, poultry, and dairy industries. And if an undocumented agricultural worker has already been living in the U.S. without legal authorization, they don't qualify to leave the U.S. and get an H2A. So, we need to fix this in order for all of the people who are currently working to grow the food to be able to stay in the U.S. and continue that important work.

The solution for this is a bill that has already been proposed in Congress, called the Farm Workforce Modernization Act. The bill would provide a legal process for current undocumented agricultural workers to apply for temporary status, which could be renewed indefinitely. This would allow them to continue working here, but legally, until they decide to stop working and return to their home country. Additionally, for long-term agricultural workers who have been here a number of years, they could apply for lawful permanent residence if they pay a $1,000 fine and continue to work in agriculture for a number of years. This bill would serve a number of purposes to help the United States. First, it would ensure that we have an agricultural workforce in the future. Second, it would require mandatory E-verify to be phased in after the government processes all of the applications for temporary status and legalization, so that there is not an undocumented workforce in the future.

Essential Workers for Economic Advancement Act

In August, 2025, the Department of Labor published a report called "America's Talent Strategy: Equipping American Workers for the Golden Age." This is a laudable effort to strengthen America's workforce, grow the economy, and help the United States continue to be an economic superpower. But, like it or not, Americans cannot do it alone. We need help. The United States has a shortage of skilled workers that requires both American workers and immigrants.

In the U.S. manufacturing industry, there is currently a shortage of workers such as welders, machinists, and technicians, with a projected need of almost 4 million new manufacturing workers in the next 10 years. There are plans to provide training for Americans to do this work. But at the same time, these manufacturing companies need skilled workers to fill the gaps right now.

In order to address this issue, Republican Congressman Lloyd Smucker of Pennsylvania has introduced a bill in Congress called the Essential Workers for Economic Advancement Act, which would add a new nonimmigrant classification, H-2C. This bill would provide an additional 65,000 visas per year for temporary workers to do nonagricultural jobs (not requiring a bachelor's degree) for which U.S. employers cannot find U.S. workers. This bill would enable U.S. companies to bring in needed workers to do a range of jobs requiring skills (but not a college degree) where there is a shortage of American workers, such as machine operators, semiconductor processing technicians, welders, electricians, construction workers, hospitality workers, and long-term caregivers.

This bill is a great start. It would require that employers recruit U.S. workers first, but if employers cannot find qualified U.S. workers, then they could bring in qualified workers from around the world to supplement the U.S. workforce on a temporary basis for 3 years. According to Congressman Smucker, this bill is supported by the U.S. Chamber of Commerce, National Association of Manufacturers, Essential Worker Immigration Coalition, Associated Builders and Contractors, Associated General Contractors, National Restaurant Association, National Roofing Contractors Association, American Hotel and Lodging Association, National Association of Home Builders, and The LIBRE Initiative. This bill would create an important legal mechanism for U.S. employers to meet the demand for workers who work in fields that require skills, but don't require a college degree.

I would suggest a few common sense improvements. In order to ensure the integrity of the program and make sure it doesn't suppress wages, it should incorporate input from labor unions as to the actual shortage of American workers and it should ensure that the wages paid to nonimmigrant workers match the prevailing wages for U.S. citizens. In addition, it should allow the temporary workers to bring their immediate family with them. We are a nation of family values. It should be obvious that a valuable worker should be able to bring a spouse and children to accompany him or her. We should also recognize that a nonimmigrant who comes to the U.S. to work and help build our country should have the ability to apply for lawful permanent residence after a number of years, as long they have followed the law, paid taxes, and contributed to the community. With these common sense changes, this bill could dramatically strengthen the United States, both in the short-term and long-term.

Immigrant Visas

Here are the immigrant visa categories, for people who qualify to get their green cards, to live in the United States permanently. There are two primary groups of people who are eligible to immigrate permanently to the U.S. and become lawful permanent residents. First, there is the family-based immigration system. Second, there is the employment-based immigration system. Together, the family-based and employment-based immigration categories are the foundation of our legal immigration system for immigrants to get green cards (lawful permanent residence). As you will see, it can be pretty complicated, and there are a number of improvements we can make to it.

Family-Immigration

Within the family-immigration system, there are two separate groups of family visas: (1) Immediate Relative of U.S. citizens, and (2) other close family members of U.S. citizens and lawful permanent residents.

Immediate Relatives of U.S. citizens (spouse, kids, & parents)

The first group of family visas is immediate family of U.S. citizens. This includes the U.S. citizen's spouse, kids, and parents. This is called "Immediate Relatives of U.S. citizens." It's important to note that there are an unlimited number of visas for immediate family members of U.S. citizens.

Other Family-Sponsored Immigrant Visas

The second group of family-based immigrants are referred to as the Family Preference Categories, for other close relatives of U.S. citizens and lawful permanent residents. As you will see, it's complicated and some of the waiting times are wild.

These family-based categories provide a limited number of visas each year for different categories: (1) adult children of U.S. citizens; (2) spouses, kids, and adult children of lawful permanent residents; and (3) brothers and sisters of U.S. citizens. Within each category, countries are limited to 7% of the total. There's one category for unmarried adult children and another category for married adult children. Those are known as Family 1st Preference and Family 3rd Preference, respectively. Then, there's also spouses and children of lawful permanent residents, which is known as Family 2nd Preference. It's F2A for spouses and kids under 21. It's F2B for unmarried adult kids 21 years old and older. Finally, there are brothers and sisters of adult U.S. citizens: this is called F4 (Family 4th Preference).

Here's the official list of the family-sponsored preference categories, as written by the government in the Department of State Visa Bulletin:

> **"FAMILY-SPONSORED PREFERENCES**
>
> **First: (F1)** Unmarried Sons and Daughters of U.S. Citizens;
>
> **Second:** Spouses and Children, and Unmarried Sons and Daughters of Permanent Residents;
>
> A. **(F2A)** Spouses and Children of Permanent Residents;
>
> B. **(F2B)** Unmarried Sons and Daughters (21 years of age or older) of Permanent Residents;
>
> **Third: (F3)** Married Sons and Daughters of U.S. Citizens; and
>
> **Fourth: (F4)** Brothers and Sisters of Adult U.S. Citizens."

All of these family preference categories have limits on the number of visas that can be given out each year, and also have limitations on the number of visas within the categories for certain countries. These limitations create long backlogs of many years for people who applied years ago and are waiting for their priority date to become current. The "priority date" is whatever date the visa petition was filed and the "current" date is kind of like the "front of the line."

The Department of State publishes a document each month known as the Visa Bulletin. The following chart is for the family-sponsored preference categories for February, 2026, as published by the Department of State's official Visa Bulletin:

Category	All Countries	China	India	Mexico	Philippines
F1	11/8/2016	11/8/16	11/8/16	12/22/06	3/1/13
F2A	2/1/2024	2/1/24	2/1/24	2/1/23	2/1/24
F2B	12/1/2016	12/1/16	12/1/16	2/15/09	12/22/12
F3	9/8/2011	9/8/11	9/8/11	5/1/01	3/1/05
F4	1/8/2008	1/8/08	11/1/06	4/8/01	7/22/06

This shows the dates on which the visa petition had to be filed for the person to finally be eligible to get a visa in February 2026. In other words, if the petition was filed on or before these dates, the person can now get a visa. If the petition was filed after these dates, the person is still waiting in line. For example, on the first line, F1 is an unmarried son or daughter of a U.S. citizen. Say a U.S. citizen filed an immigration petition for a 21 year old son or daughter 20 years ago, in September 2006 (for the sake of this example, assume the son or daughter was born in Mexico). The "current date" for F-1 Mexico is December 22, 2006. That means that if the petition was filed before December 22, 2006, that then-21-year-old child whose U.S. citizen parent filed for him or her in 2006 (who is now 41 years old in 2026) has been waiting for the last 20 years and is just now finally able to get a visa.

Let's look at another example. Under the F2A category for Mexico, if a lawful permanent resident filed for his or her spouse or child under the age of 21 in February 2023, they've been waiting three years to be eligible to finally get a visa. It also means that right now, if the lawful permanent resident files an immigration petition for his or her 20-year-old son or daughter in 2026, the kid won't get the visa before he or she turns 21 because of the three-year backlog. And then, by turning 21 while waiting for the visa, the child "ages out" and gets put into the F2B category (unmarried kids over 21 of lawful permanent residents). The F2B line is much longer. For F2B Mexico, the "front of the line" where people are now eligible to get visas are the adult kids of permanent residents whose parents filed for them 17 years ago, on or before February 15, 2009. So the result is that after the kid turns 21, it's probably going to be another 16 years of waiting! These are examples of how the system is broken because these waiting times are so long that it defeats the purpose of family unification.

A common sense solution would be to recognize that spouses and children under the age of 21 of lawful permanent residents should be given priority for family unification and take this category out of the preference-based system. This would allow spouses and kids of lawful permanent residents to process their applications without long waiting times and without the possibility of kids "aging out." This would also help eliminate the logjam that currently exists for the other categories by freeing up visa numbers for other categories. This type of reform has already been proposed in a bill called the Reuniting Families Act, introduced by Congresswoman Judy Chu.

Another major problem with the current immigration laws is that even if someone qualifies to become a lawful permanent resident, there are many other sections of the law that can disqualify a person for one reason or another. For example, if a person entered the U.S. without a visa, they are not eligible to adjust their status to that of lawful permanent resident (without leaving), unless they've been here since before December 20, 2000, and someone filed an immigration petition for them prior to April 30, 2001. This is the law of Section 245(a) and 245(i), respectively. If they qualify for their green card, but can't do it in the U.S. through adjustment of status, they would have to leave and apply for an immigrant visa outside the U.S. This would be fine, *if it was possible.*

But what makes it impossible for most immigrants to do this is known as the "3 & 10-year bars." Under the current immigration laws, if someone has resided in the U.S. unlawfully for at least six months (but less than one year of being here unlawfully), and then that person leaves the U.S., they can't come back for at least 3 years. This is the 3 year bar. The 10 year bar, on the other hand, is if someone has been in the U.S. unlawfully for at least one year and then departs, they are ineligible for a visa or green card for 10 years.

The current immigration laws also contain an anomaly for how the 10-year bar applies to noncitizens who were brought to the U.S. as children. The law makes it so that, if the person was a child under the age of 18, it does not apply to them so long as they were only unlawfully present in the U.S. for less than 1 year. But if a noncitizen was in the U.S. unlawfully for more than one year as a child and then left and came back, even still as a child, then that person is ineligible for a visa or green card unless and until they spend at least 10 years outside the U.S. This has had an effect on real people's lives, where someone was brought to the U.S. as a child, then after being here for more than a year, that child is taken back to Mexico for a short trip and returns to the U.S. again as a child, without a visa. Many years later as an adult, after spending most of their life in the U.S., they might qualify for a green card. But because of that one time when they were taken out of the U.S. as a child and then brought back, they will be barred unless they decide to give up their life here to go live in Mexico for 10 years. For a person in their forties who has only ever known the U.S., this is not only unrealistic but cruel.

Employment-based immigrant visas

The law currently authorizes 140,000 visas per year for all employment-based immigrant visas. There are 5 preference categories for employment-based immigrant visas. The First Preference is called "EB-1," for people with extraordinary ability, outstanding researchers, and multinational corporate leaders. The Second Preference is "EB-2," for highly educated professionals holding advanced degrees or people who have exceptional technical ability. The Third Preference is "EB-3," for skilled workers and specialists. The Fourth Preference is "EB-4," for special immigrants, such as religious workers. The Fifth Preference is "EB-5," which is for wealthy immigrant investors. Within each of these categories, there is a per-country cap of 7% so that no single country can have more than 7% of the visas.

The problem with the employment-based immigrant visas is that the current immigration laws are written in a way that cause tremendous backlogs. These end up hurting American businesses, because they are the ones petitioning for these workers. It also hurts Americans in general because the employment-based immigrant visas are designed to bring in specialized labor that we need in such professions as health care, like physical therapists and professional nurses. The United States needs more workers in these fields. There are many people who have already been approved by USCIS for employment-based immigrant visas, but they can't get the visas because of the limited number. This has created backlogs with waiting times of many years. In many cases, these are the best of the best of the world, but we don't have enough visa numbers for all of them.

There are a couple reasons for these backlogs. AILA and the American Immigration Council have noted that one problem with the current system is the way we count visas and green cards. In the Immigration Act of 1990, Congress set a cap on the total number of immigrant visas or green cards that can be issued for all the categories. This cap is 226,000 for family members of U.S. citizens and lawful permanent residents, 140,000 for employment-based immigrant petitions, and 55,000 for diversity lottery winners. These limits were meant to be the actual number of principal immigrants (not including their own family members). So, for example, we should be getting 140,000 talented workers each year to help grow our economy. But instead, the Department of State interprets this to mean that 140,000 is the cap on the total number of all visas for workers and their own families. The effect of this is that only about 60% of the visas get used for their intended purpose of going to the actual immigrant workers. The other 40% of the visas, approximately, are used up by the families of the immigrant workers. The family members are called "derivatives." We should change the law so that "derivative" family members are not counted against the cap.

This matters because it defeats the purpose of Congress allotting those 140,000 visas for workers in the first place. The employment-based immigration categories are not there to make us feel good. The employment-based immigration categories are there to help U.S. businesses bring in needed workers.

We can make America stronger if we make a few changes. For example, the Dignity Act would stop the government from counting family members against the cap on employment-based visa numbers, thereby freeing up visa numbers for workers who have already been approved by USCIS, but who are waiting years for their visas. It's important to note that the Dignity Act does not add to the number of visas allocated each year to immigrant workers. Instead, it just makes the law more efficient at serving our societal needs. This is an example of how the immigration laws can be changed to grow the economy of the U.S.

Immigrants Support Our Military

When immigrants give their sons and daughters to the military, there is an immigration "program," so to speak, that allows USCIS to give the parents or spouse of the military service member something called "Military Parole In Place." If a military service member's spouse or parent came to the U.S. illegally, without a visa, then USCIS may grant them temporary lawful status which makes it possible to apply and receive a green card based on either spousal relationship or the parent/child relationship. Otherwise, if that person was not in the military or a veteran, they could still apply for their spouse or parent, but the spouse or parent would not be able to adjust their status in the U.S. if they had entered the U.S. without a visa. They would be subject to the 10 year bar by leaving the U.S. to apply for a visa abroad.

I was never in the military, but I greatly admire, respect, and appreciate those who serve. It is a calling that some people have, and some people don't. I hope that everyone who reads this book would agree that those of us who don't have that calling greatly appreciate the sacrifices of those who do. This point is somewhat obvious. But it's important to recognize what kind of people we are. We're people who honor our military and military families. We don't take them for granted. We know that they have made all sorts of sacrifices for our benefit. We owe a great debt to the spouses and parents of military members.

So it's only fitting that we try to make immigration easier for military service members' spouses and parents.

But here's the problem. Although this program has helped lots of families, there are many others whom it hasn't helped because immigration law is such a mess. Here are some of the reasons people will not qualify for this program, even if their spouse or child is in the military. Number 1, if you have a case in immigration court, you don't qualify. Number 2, if you came to the U.S. without a visa, and ever went back for any reason, such as to visit family, and then re-entered the U.S. a second time, you trigger the bar and don't qualify. The first one can sometimes be fixed if you can get DHS to agree to drop the deportation case. But the second one, there's no reprieve. A person born in the 1970s who came to the U.S. in the 1990s, and then maybe in the early 2000s went back to Mexico to see a sick relative and came back to the U.S. to resume their life here, and now has a child in the military... that person's out of luck. This law is harsh and unforgiving. If you have it, it sticks to you and there's nothing you can do unless you leave the U.S. for 10 years. The unintended effect of this law is that it creates a giant group of immigrants who stand no chance of "doing it the right way."

A person might give their child to this country, and still not be eligible to have legal status. This is yet another reason why we need to eliminate Section 212(a)(9)(B) and (C) from the immigration laws, to get rid of the 3 & 10-year bars.

Common Sense Legal Fixes

General Waiver of Inadmissibility

One of the many immigration reform ideas talked about by Ira Kurzban, one of the preeminent immigration lawyers in the U.S., is to have a general waiver of inadmissibility. There are over 30 different reasons a person might be disqualified from getting a visa or green card to the U.S. and thereby ineligible for lawful permanent residence. Some of the grounds of inadmissibility have waivers, and some do not. Of the ones that have waivers available, not everyone qualifies. For example, a waiver might require that the person applying for the waiver have their own spouse or parent who is a U.S. citizen or permanent resident in order to qualify for the waiver. But if the person is in their forties or fifties and is married to another undocumented immigrant, and both of the parents are in Mexico, that person won't qualify for the waiver because they have kids who are U.S. citizens, but not parents who are U.S. citizens. And since they're married to each other (and not to a U.S. citizen) they don't have the right qualifying relative to qualify for the waiver. This makes no sense. We should make a general waiver for any ground of inadmissibility to give discretion to an immigration officer to grant the person's case if it seems appropriate. Remember, we're trying to fix the immigration laws here, and this is a reasonable solution to a problem that immigrants face even if they qualify for their green card. If someone qualifies, we should give the immigration officer the power to make the call and let them in.

10 Year Statute of Limitations

Another change we need to make (also Mr. Kurzban's idea) is to have a Statute of Limitations in immigration law. As Americans, we have all grown up with the idea of "statute of limitations." The idea is that if somebody did something wrong, then there's a finite time period to hold it against them. If you're in a car accident, there's a statute of limitations that says how long you have to file a lawsuit. If you commit a crime, there's usually a statute of limitations for the state to bring charges, unless it was something like murder. I think we Americans love statutes of limitations.

Why can't we have the same thing for immigration? The way it is right now, immigration law is full of things that make it perpetually harder or impossible for immigrants to "do it the right way" because the law has harsh consequences for things that were done a long time ago. The classic case is if a person made even the slightest misrepresentation about something, no matter how long ago it was. In the case where someone was convicted of a crime, even a misdemeanor, these things can prevent people from getting their green card even if they happened twenty or thirty years ago.

I would like to propose that we should be more forgiving. I'm not talking about forgiving murderers. I'm talking about if someone is now in their forties, and they did a minor crime or lied about something 10 or 20 years ago, we shouldn't necessarily deny their green card. We could have a 10-year statute of limitations so that if something happened more than 10 years ago that was not a serious crime, we won't hold it against them.

Statute of Limitations on Old Removal Orders

As of 2025, there were approximately 1.5 million people in the United States who had already lost their immigration court case and were ordered deported by an immigration judge. Some of these old removal orders are 10-20 years old, or longer. Think of this as a civil judgment. Many of these people lost their cases simply because the immigration law doesn't give them a way to stay in the U.S., not because they are undesirable. In many states, a civil judgment must be executed within a certain time period, or it lapses. The legal principle is called laches. Basically, if a person sits on their rights, then they lose those rights. What if it's the government that sits on their rights? Although the Supreme Court has held that laches cannot be raised as a defense against the federal government, we might consider if the immigration law should be changed to reflect laches as a moral principle.

In the immigration context, if a noncitizen lost their immigration case many years ago, but the government did not make them leave and the person has still been living in the U.S. for the last 10-20 years, or more, we might ask ourselves if that civil judgment for deportation should still be enforceable. For example, if a noncitizen was ordered deported twenty years ago or more, and the government did nothing about it, should the government still be able to now pluck the person off the street and ship them off? There are many cases where the government waited many years, throughout several different administrations, and did not deport them. Meanwhile, the person with a deportation order has been raising a family of U.S. citizen kids and contributing to the community. We should re-examine if it's in the best interests of the United States to still deport them.

I would suggest that immigration law should be reformed to have a statute of limitations on old removal orders from more than 10 years ago. This would not be amnesty. Rather, it would mean that if the government wants to now deport a person with an old removal order, they should reopen the case and determine if it's still in the best interests of the United States for that person to be deported. If the noncitizen has family here and has never been convicted of a crime, they should be given an opportunity to apply for whatever relief from deportation they might be eligible for now, such as Registry.

All in the Family

The final miscellaneous change is how we define marriage. Gay marriage has been legal in the United States for more than ten years. Since the Supreme Court recognized same-sex marriage nationwide in the case of *Obergefell v. Hodges* in 2015, the U.S. government has also recognized it in the way it interprets immigration laws. This means that right now, a gay spouse from another country can immigrate to the United States to live with their American spouse as an "Immediate Relative" of a U.S. citizen. This is a beautiful example of family values: we fully appreciate the love that two people can have for each other. We should be happy to see that love, and we should want to celebrate it. A lot of people immigrate to the United States because they fall in love with an American and the American falls in love with them, and they want to be together. Fortunately for us, these married couples want to build their lives right here in the U.S.

I propose that we take this opportunity to codify gay marriage. Gay couples are just as committed, patient, and kind as straight couples are. Since the government already recognizes gay marriage, we're not adding anything new. We're just writing it down in the law so everybody knows that this is something we agree on, that we value all families.

If we make these common sense changes to our legal immigration system, we can take a giant leap for humanity and for our country as a world leader. We can continue to have a reliable food supply. We can grow our economy through legal immigration. And we can ensure that families stay together. We need to give the government the ability to grant legal immigration status to the many immigrants who are not violent people, who are deeply-rooted in our communities, and who work alongside Americans. These common sense fixes not only help our economy, but also can put an end to these people being incarcerated in immigration jails for no reason other than the current law doesn't have the protections for them that it should.

CHAPTER 9

Anyone Can Become an American

THAT'S WHAT RONALD REAGAN SAID. No matter what corner of the world you come from, you can become an American. Think how different that is from other countries. We are the only country in the world where immigrants can transform themselves from being from some other country to being "of" the United States. When a person goes through the naturalization process, they become a United States citizen and thereby become American. It's often a long, winding, arduous road to get there. Along the way, they sometimes feel rejected by our country in different ways, but once they get there, U.S. citizenship is the ultimate membership in a special club. It is an achievement that people are rightfully proud of. Naturalized U.S. citizens often say, "The United States is the greatest country in the world."

Let's talk about how a person becomes a U.S. citizen. First, they have to be a lawful permanent resident of the U.S. That means they have to get a green card first. After a person has been a lawful permanent resident for five years, they can apply for naturalization to become a U.S. citizen. (If they're married to a U.S. citizen, they can apply after three years.) To qualify for naturalization to become a U.S. citizen, a permanent resident has to be a person of good moral character for the past 5 years and has to be able to read, write, and speak English.

The "good moral character" requirement says that to qualify to naturalize and become a U.S. citizen, a lawful permanent resident has to have been a person of good moral character for the last five years before they apply. This statutory 5-year look-back period under Section 316(a) of the INA recognizes that isolated infractions in the past should not disqualify a person from naturalization, if the individual has demonstrated rehabilitation. So an immigrant doesn't have to be a perfect person with a spotless record to be a U.S. citizen (most U.S. citizens are not perfect, after all). By the way, most immigrants don't have a checkered past, but the point is, there's room for them if they stay out of trouble.

A naturalization applicant also has to pass a civics test about U.S. history and government. The naturalization civics test is made up of 128 questions. At the interview, the immigration officer asks the person 20 questions (picked randomly from the 128), and the applicant has to answer at least 12 questions correctly.

Here's a sample test of 20 naturalization questions, with the official answers from the U.S. government. In some cases, there's more than one acceptable right answer. These questions and answers are reproduced directly from the government's own official U.S. Citizenship and Immigration Services (USCIS) 2025 Civics Test standard handbook.

1. What is the supreme law of the land?
    - (U.S.) Constitution
2. Who lived in America before the Europeans arrived?
    - American Indians
    - Native Americans
3. What group of people was taken and sold as slaves?
    - Africans
    - People from Africa

4. What did the Emancipation Proclamation do?
    - Freed the slaves
    - Freed slaves in the Confederacy
    - Freed slaves in the Confederate states
    - Freed slaves in most Southern states
5. What did the civil rights movement do?
    - Fought to end racial discrimination
6. The U.S. Constitution starts with the words "We the People." What does "We the People" mean?
    - Self-government
    - Popular sovereignty
    - Consent of the governed
    - People should govern themselves
    - (Example of) social contract
7. What is the rule of law?
    - Everyone must follow the law.
    - Leaders must obey the law.
    - Government must obey the law.
    - No one is above the law.
8. There are three branches of government. Why?
    - So one part does not become too powerful
    - Checks and balances
    - Separation of powers
9. What amendment says all persons born or naturalized in the United States, and subject to the jurisdiction thereof, are U.S. citizens?
    - 14th Amendment
10. What do we show loyalty to when we say the Pledge of Allegiance?
    - The United States
    - The flag

11. The colonists came to America for many reasons. Name one.
    - Freedom
    - Political liberty
    - Religious freedom
    - Economic opportunity
    - Escape persecution
12. The President of the United States can serve only two terms. Why?
    - (Because of) the 22nd Amendment
    - To keep the president from becoming too powerful
13. Why is the Electoral College important?
    - It decides who is elected president.
    - It provides a compromise between the popular election of the president and congressional selection.
14. What does the judicial branch do?
    - Reviews laws
    - Explains laws
    - Resolves disputes (disagreements) about the law
    - Decides if a law goes against the (U.S.) Constitution
15. How many seats are on the Supreme Court?
    - Nine
16. What stops one branch of government from becoming too powerful?
    - checks and balances
    - separation of powers
17. Name one power that is only for the states.
    - Provide schooling and education
    - Provide protection (police)
    - Provide safety (fire departments)
    - Give a driver's license
    - Approve zoning and land use

18. What is the purpose of the 10th Amendment?
    - (It states that the) powers not given to the federal government belong to the states or to the people.
19. What are three rights of everyone living in the United States?
    - Freedom of expression
    - Freedom of speech
    - Freedom of assembly
    - Freedom to petition the government
    - Freedom of religion
    - The right to bear arms
20. Name two promises that new citizens make in the Oath of Allegiance.
    - Give up loyalty to other countries
    - Defend the (U.S.) Constitution
    - Obey the laws of the United States
    - Serve in the military (if needed)
    - Serve (help, do important work for) the nation (if needed)
    - Be loyal to the United States

I have attended many naturalization interviews with clients. They have the right to have an attorney present, but they're on their own when it comes to answering these civics questions. I admire the fact that many people have not only learned a second language, but also learned the most significant things about our country. Can you imagine going to another country where you don't speak the language, and then learning the language and also memorizing 128 of the most important things about their history and their government? I think it's pretty impressive.

The Oath of Allegiance

When a person immigrates to the United States and finally gets to be a U.S. citizen, there's a ceremony. They recite The Oath of Allegiance to the United States. This is a solemn event which everyone takes very seriously, including the USCIS officers who conduct the ceremony, the immigrant who is taking the oath, and the immigrant's friends and family who come to witness it. Let's take a look at The Oath of Allegiance:

> *"I hereby declare, on oath, that I absolutely and entirely renounce and abjure all allegiance and fidelity to any foreign prince, potentate, state, or sovereignty, of whom or which I have heretofore been a subject or citizen; that I will support and defend the Constitution and laws of the United States of America against all enemies, foreign and domestic;*
>
> *that I will bear true faith and allegiance to the same;*
>
> *that I will bear arms on behalf of the United States when required by the law;*
>
> *that I will perform noncombatant service in the Armed Forces of the United States when required by the law;*
>
> *that I will perform work of national importance under civilian direction when required by the law;*
>
> *and that I take this obligation freely without any mental reservation or purpose of evasion."*

The only thing that someone can change and say differently is, if they have a religious objection to war, they don't have to say "bear arms." But otherwise, these are the words someone must say aloud when they become a U.S. citizen.

The idea of the Oath goes all the way back to the first naturalization law in 1790, which required immigrants to take an oath to support the Constitution. The exact, actual words of the whole

Oath have changed over time. The current text of the Oath is formally codified in the regulations at 8 C.F.R. § 337.1. The Oath as it is written right now and recited by immigrants when they become U.S. citizens is strongly worded. I believe that a person saying these words is making a choice. Imagine that you have come from another country and are saying these words about the United States. When an immigrant says these words, they are drawing a stark contrast between their allegiance to the United States, an exalted place where they have achieved their dream of U.S. citizenship, versus the nostalgia they have for the country they left. By reciting these words, the naturalization applicant affirmatively assumes the full constitutional responsibilities of citizenship and is pledging allegiance to the United States.

As mentioned earlier, the general rule is that an immigrant needs to become a lawful permanent resident (LPR) and then, after being an LPR for at least 5 years, they can apply for Naturalization to become a U.S. citizen. I would propose we make an exception for Dreamers. They grew up here speaking English and learning U.S. civics in school, so they are already as American as anybody. As children, they pledged allegiance to the flag and to the Republic for which it stands. We should give Dreamers a fast track to Naturalization. After a Dreamer becomes a lawful permanent resident, we should change the law to let them apply for Naturalization after just 3 years of being an LPR. This is the same exception we make for spouses of U.S. citizens. A Dreamer is practically American already by virtue of growing up in the U.S. and completing high school or a GED. If ever a person was "just like us," it's a Dreamer. We should allow them to become Americans.

CHAPTER 10

The First Amendment

OUR NATION WAS FOUNDED 250 years ago with our Declaration of Independence from a king. Our forefathers, who incidentally were either immigrants or the descendants of immigrants themselves, instilled within us the belief that we have the right to self-governance. Eleven years later, in 1787, they wrote the Constitution to form the government that we still have today. They amended the Constitution with the first ten amendments known as the Bill of Rights, including, of course, the First Amendment. As everyone knows, the First Amendment contains the right to freedom of speech.

The ICE enforcement operations starting in 2025 made a lot of American citizens upset with what their government was doing, causing many to speak out against the government. As many others have stated, there is so much at stake, not just for immigrants, but also for people born and raised in the United States of America to continue to live freely. It's worth remembering what Americans have been so upset about. These ICE enforcement operations have caused many Americans to have strong negative feelings about the ICE agency as a whole and has caused Americans to ask fundamental questions about the nature of ICE and how it should enforce immigration law. Before getting into those issues, it's important to look back at what happened to understand why so many Americans have been so outraged that they took to the streets to voice their opposition to the way the government has been enforcing immigration law.

One of the first well-publicized incidents took place on March 25, 2025, when ICE agents arrested a Tufts University doctoral student on the street as part of a visa revocation process in response to her op-ed regarding Israel and Gaza. Many Americans were shocked to see the nearby surveillance video of the arrest. The image of ICE officers appearing out of nowhere to put handcuffs on this woman and whisk her off was deeply unsettling. She wasn't dangerous and the arrest seemed to be retaliation against her exercising her First Amendment rights which all people in the United States have. She was later released from ICE custody through a petition for habeas corpus and her removal proceedings were terminated.

Around the same time, ICE arrested noncitizens under the Alien Enemies Act and deported a number of people to El Salvador to the notorious CECOT prison, based on alleged gang affiliation even though some of the men did not seem to be the dangerous gang members that the government would have us believe. It shocked the conscience that the government deported a man to El Salvador to be locked up in CECOT even though he had been granted withholding of removal by an immigration judge which should have legally protected him from being deported to El Salvador. The Supreme Court later ruled that the government had to facilitate his return to the U.S.

In May 2025, the government began to arrest people at their immigration court hearings. This seemed underhanded and unjust because these were immigrants who were going to court to apply for asylum, only to have the immigration judges dismiss their cases so that ICE could then arrest them in the hallway or outside the courthouse and put them into a process called expedited removal.

In June 2025, ICE and the Border Patrol began conducting immigration raids in Los Angeles in which masked officers suddenly arrested immigrants off the street. Most of the immigrants who were arrested did not have any criminal history. Many of the arrests were the result of racial profiling. The government's immigration enforcement operations did not appear to be for the purpose of keeping Americans safe, such as if they had focused on arresting immigrants with convictions for violent crimes. Rather, it appeared to be an obvious show of strength by the federal government against the city of Los Angeles. People viewed the federal government's actions not as keeping the community safe but rather as an attack on the community. The people of Los Angeles highly objected to this type of immigration law enforcement and loudly protested. The government doubled-down on this enforcement operation by deploying the National Guard and sending in the Marines.

In July 2025, ICE and CBP raided a cannabis farm near Oxnard, California, and arrested a young man who was on his way to his job as a security guard there. The man identified himself to officers as a U.S. citizen and an Army veteran, and told them he was going to work. Nevertheless, agents tear-gassed him, pepper-sprayed him, dragged him out of his vehicle, arrested him, and held him in custody for 3 days before being released without charges.

In September 2025, ICE continued their "crackdown" in Boston and Chicago. Some of the immigration arrests appeared to be agents walking up to random, brown-skinned people and asking where they were born. Others were so-called "targeted" operations to arrest immigrants who were living peacefully in the community but may have had civil immigration law violations. Chicago residents responded by protesting outside the ICE facility in Broadview, Illinois, and agents were seen tear-gassing the protesters in violation of their First Amendment rights. Finally, ICE literally descended upon a Chicago apartment building from a helicopter, arresting 37 immigrants and detaining several U.S. citizens for hours.

In Portland, the administration attempted to portray the city as "war-ravaged," in order to justify deploying National Guard troops in response to protesters. The supposed legal justification was that there was an "invasion, rebellion, or inability to execute federal law." A federal judge ruled against the administration and blocked the administration from using the National Guard against protests. The judge said that describing the city as "war-ravaged" was "untethered to the facts." The protests were not an insurrection, but rather an exercise of free speech under the First Amendment.

In November, masked agents moved to Charlotte and arrested hundreds of immigrants there. They followed this in December by going to New Orleans, where they justified the show of force by saying that noncitizens who had been arrested, but not convicted, of crimes were terrorizing the city and that large numbers of agents were necessary for officer safety.

Americans across the country intensely criticized these actions by the federal government. People did not want to see ICE arresting immigrants as they were going to work and taking their kids to school, regardless of whether someone might have entered the United States illegally. Americans intuitively know that it's fundamentally wrong to have masked law enforcement officers arresting noncriminal people with no notice, no hearing, and no moral justification. In neighborhoods of cities such as Los Angeles, Chicago, and Minneapolis, Americans witnessed masked ICE agents stop immigrants and violently remove them from their vehicles. Officers interrogated U.S. citizens even. And hundreds of thousands of U.S. citizen children have now been separated from a parent arrested by ICE. Ordinary Americans protested ICE because the manner in which ICE was enforcing the law seemed harsh to the point of being un-American. Americans attempted to warn their immigrant neighbors of ICE presence and they protested against this ICE activity. This all culminated in great misfortune, when DHS sent its officers and agents to Minneapolis in January 2026 resulting in the deaths of Renee Good and Alex Pretti. After these two deaths, ICE changed its tactics to be less high-profile in arresting immigrants, but no less intent on mass deportations of immigrants who pose no danger or threat to society. These are the reasons that many Americans have called to "abolish ICE," or, at the very least, reform ICE.

Immigration officers should not be in a position where they feel pitted against U.S. citizens who are protesting the manner in which the government is enforcing the civil immigration laws. The problem is not that U.S. citizens hate law enforcement. By and large U.S. citizens support law enforcement. But U.S. citizens do have strong negative feelings about the way ICE and Border Patrol have been enforcing immigration laws by their haphazard sweeps through the community and the government's violent reaction to dissent. U.S. citizens also object to masked government agents arresting immigrants who are living peacefully in the community, regardless of whether they may have civil immigration violations. If the government wants to send immigrants to immigration court, the government can give them a Notice to Appear. But U.S. citizens do not wish to see noncitizens arrested by ICE simply for being unlawfully present in the United States.

The following chapters contain proposals for how we can change the institution of ICE while still having civil immigration law enforcement in the United States, and how we can change the enforcement of the law to make it more civil and humane.

CHAPTER 11

A Plan for ICE

FIRST OF ALL, LET ME just say that there are good ICE officers. I know some of them personally. So even though there are currently ICE enforcement policies that are harming people and videos abound of ICE officers doing horrible things to immigrants and U.S. citizens alike (including excessive force, and even killing people), I do not generalize that all ICE officers are bad. Several things can be true at once, that there are some good ICE officers, that there is overzealous immigration law enforcement, and that the organization of ICE needs serious reform.

If you, the reader, have a family member who works for ICE and that person is one of the good ones, then please know that my criticism of ICE does not apply to them personally or professionally. If they are one of the good ones, then we should all assume that they are as honorable at work as they are at home. The criticism of ICE in the following pages is not meant to diminish the reputation of these good people who have had careers working for ICE where they have treated people with dignity and respect.

Let's talk about the history of the Immigration and Naturalization Service. INS started as a government agency under the Department of Labor in 1933. In 1940, INS became part of the

Department of Justice, and it continued to be part of the Department of Justice from 1940 until 2003. During that time, up until 2003, people used to apply for their green cards and citizenship at INS. INS was also in charge of immigration law enforcement in the interior of the United States.

On September 11, 2001, the United States suffered devastating terrorist attacks. In response to the terrorist attacks, Congress created the Department of Homeland Security in 2003 and INS was abolished. INS's functions were split into three new agencies within DHS: (1) Immigration and Customs Enforcement (ICE for interior civil immigration enforcement and criminal investigations); (2) U.S. Citizenship and Immigration Services (USCIS for immigration benefits); and (3) U.S. Customs and Border Protection (CBP for customs and border protection).

Everyone agreed that we should have security against terrorism, but there was some disagreement over how we should go about it. Some people, such as Senator Russ Feingold, didn't think the creation of DHS was such a great idea because they foresaw the possibility of it leading to government abuse and "mission creep." Senator Feingold warned that the creation of DHS might lead to there being a personal police force of the President, allowing for the violation of both citizens' and non-citizens' Constitutional rights under the Fourth and Fifth Amendment. At the time, those who supported the creation of DHS thought that the idea of a President abusing his power in a such a way was so unlikely and absurd that it should not be taken seriously. In fact, Paul Rosenzweig, who went on to become the Deputy Assistant Secretary for Policy at DHS, has stated that they "pooh-poohed it." But Mr. Rosenzweig has now acknowledged that some of Senator Feingold's concerns have come true.

DHS Today

DHS has several important operational components. Here's a quick overview of DHS as it stands now: FEMA (disaster response and recovery), TSA (airport & transportation security), CISA (cybersecurity and infrastructure protection), U.S. Coast Guard, the U.S. Secret Service, USCIS (immigration benefit adjudications, such as green cards), CBP (border, ports, and trade enforcement), and ICE (immigration enforcement and international crime investigations).

Within ICE, there are two separate law enforcement arms: (1) Homeland Security Investigations (HSI) (which does criminal law enforcement) and (2) Enforcement and Removal Operations (ERO) (which does civil immigration law enforcement).

It's also important to highlight some of the public benefits of ICE as an organization. HSI does actual criminal law investigations and enforcement, such as transnational organized crime, drug smuggling, human trafficking, fraud, money laundering and financial crimes, cybercrime and terrorism-related cases. Obviously, HSI law enforcement is vital to public safety and national security. ERO handles interior enforcement of immigration laws, such as arresting, detaining, and deporting noncitizens for civil immigration offenses.

Throughout the years, ICE Enforcement and Removal Operations (ERO) has been the organization in charge of deporting immigrants. For most of that time, ICE/ERO attempted to balance the public safety concern of deporting immigrants with criminal convictions against the recognition that undocumented immigrants without criminal convictions did not raise those same concerns. Starting in 2004, ICE implemented the Alternatives to Detention (ATD) Program for the supervised release and monitoring of immigrants who have cases in immigration court but who are not public safety threats or flight risks. ICE has operated the ATD program for over 20 years. In addition, prior to 2017, ICE leadership implemented prosecutorial discretion to prioritize the deportation of immigrants with serious criminal convictions, instead of noncitizens without any criminal history. From January 2016 to June 2017, ICE also operated the Family Case Management Program (FCMP) which was a program designed to ensure that families with children who had to attend immigration court showed up for court, without the need to hold them in immigration detention centers. In addition, it should be noted that prior to 2025, there was a strong institutional recognition within ICE of the importance of not mistakenly detaining U.S. citizens. These are all examples of responsible, humane policies to enforce the civil immigration laws prior to 2025.

Why Reform ICE

ICE was once a respected agency, not necessarily known for abuse. Prior to 2025, most ICE agents tried to do their jobs with professionalism. Many still do. But the agency has become tarnished. It has recently been given a mission of mass deportations that is inconsistent with American values. It has put Americans in danger, and even killed people. Since January 2025, there have been at least 170 documented allegations of U.S. citizens being unlawfully detained by ICE. There have also been 2 lawsuits alleging that U.S. citizens have been deported. Not to mention the hundreds of thousands of arrests of immigrants for civil immigration violations but no criminal history, arrested without any determination of whether they pose public safety or flight risk concerns. In other words, without due process.

ICE has violated citizens' and noncitizens' Fourth Amendment right against unreasonable searches and seizures by stopping people and interrogating them based on the color of their skin. ICE has violated citizens' and noncitizens' Fifth Amendment right to due process by arresting them and incarcerating them without hearings. ICE has also violated people's First Amendment right to free speech by pepper-spraying and tear-gassing peaceful protesters who legitimately object to the cruel and barbaric manner in which ICE has enforced the immigration law starting in 2025. ICE has even killed American citizens.

Obviously, we need a government agency in charge of the civil enforcement of our civil immigration laws. But the problem with ICE in 2026 is that they cite the current immigration laws as their authority, but also often refuse to be constrained by the law. For example, on January 28, 2026, a federal judge chastised ICE for refusing to follow lawful orders at least 96 times in just January 2026 alone. We cannot have an agency that thinks the Constitution does not apply to them, which refuses to follow Court orders, and just does as it pleases. To defy judicial oversight is to go against the "checks and balances" that we were told were the foundation of our government. Law enforcement agencies should respect federal judges' orders.

Furthermore, even though ICE has changed its tactics recently to be slightly less in the spotlight, the agency still operates as if they have the last word on what the law is. This was highlighted during a June 2, 2026, Senate hearing. When Senator Chris Murphy asked the new Secretary of Homeland Security, Markwayne Mullin, if he would commit to DHS abiding by federal court orders, Secretary Mullin refused to directly answer the question. Senator Murphy politely asked him, "Can you commit to us that if a court judges something ICE is doing, something DHS is doing as illegal – unconstitutional – tells you to stop that – you will comply with the court order?" Secretary Mullin said, "I will tell you that we will never break the Constitution, and we're not going to break the law. . ." Senator Murphy pressed him on whether he would implement court orders. Secretary Mullin explained, "If we didn't think that... if we didn't think courts were politicized, then I would probably be able to answer that..." This suggests that Secretary Mullin thinks that his belief that court decisions are influenced by politics gives DHS the right to decline to follow court orders. Senator Murphy asked more time, "Will you or will you not?" And Secretary Mullin dug in and said, "I am going to enforce the law, and I'll never break the Constitution."

One of the cornerstones of our jurisprudence (and possibly our civilization) is the principle of checks and balances. Checks and balances means that federal judges are empowered to state definitively what the law is and how it applies in a case. This is a check on the Executive branch to make sure it doesn't get too powerful. This is not my opinion. As you might recall from Chapter 8, this is actually the answer to a question on the naturalization civics exam:

> What stops one branch of government from becoming too powerful?
>
> - checks and balances
> - separation of powers

Everyone agrees we should have security. We will always endeavor to keep ourselves safe. But we can do it differently than we've been doing it. Now that we are twenty-plus years into it, we can say that we've learned some things and have decided to go in a different direction with ICE.

This is an opportunity to fix the agency and make immigration law enforcement respectable again. Good ICE officers who are working to protect Americans and who are not engaged in abuses should not be seen by Americans as part of a questionable organization.

If ICE were to be re-organized, one of the first questions is, where do you move HSI? Even before the ICE controversies in 2025 and 2026, Congressman Robert Garcia proposed a bill in 2024 called the ICE Security Reform Act that would move HSI to a separate, stand-alone law enforcement agency with its own Senate-confirmed Director. According to Congressman Garcia, one of the reasons HSI needs to be separated from ICE is to ensure that it stays focused on criminal investigations to maintain public safety and national security, and to make sure that its agents do not get pulled into civil immigration enforcement operations. If this had already been done prior to 2025, it would have prevented HSI officers from being detailed to work on the ICE immigration raids. Congressman Garcia's proposal was to move the entirety of HSI to its own agency, in order to maintain continuity of ongoing investigations. HSI would continue to be part of DHS, but it would be an agency more akin to the FBI (the criminal law enforcement arm of the Department of Justice). This is important because any kind of reform needs to ensure that we continue to have strong criminal law enforcement. I would propose that the ICE Security Reform Act be incorporated as the first step to any ICE reform, to make sure that we continue to protect ourselves.

Once you make HSI its own law enforcement agency, then we can talk about what to do with the rest of ICE, such as Enforcement and Removal Operations (ERO).

The New INS

I propose that we re-create the Immigration and Naturalization Service (INS) and put it in charge of civil immigration enforcement again, but with new rules, to ensure that they have the tools to keep Americans safe and also to ensure that the immigration laws are fairly enforced, without abuse. I propose that the new

INS be part of the Department of Justice again, so that its leadership reports to the Attorney General.

The New INS would initially be made up of ICE/ERO officers who started duty before January 20, 2025 (the day of President Trump's second Inauguration). If someone began their career with ICE/ERO before January 20, 2025, we should assume that they passed a background check and received sufficient training to do their job without violating the Constitution. So, if a person started with ICE/ERO prior to that day, then they would be "grandfathered in" to INS.

If we're going to have any semblance of a fresh start and have trust in immigration law enforcement officers again, we cannot allow it to be tainted with people who were not properly vetted and trained. It is now well-known that ICE officers who started on or after January 20, 2025, were not all vetted appropriately. They were not required to pass a background check before being given a badge and a gun. Also, they did not all have sufficient training. DHS has been in such a rush to get people hired and onto the street that they let them loose onto the public without teaching them how to treat people with civility and respect. These new hires also did not get training in how to enforce the immigration law without violating people's Constitutional rights, which has led to so many abuses. On the contrary, many were told that they were exempt from rules, and were "untouchable." For this reason, any ICE/ERO officer whose initial start day was on or after January 20, 2025, would need to undergo a background check and complete new training if they wish to be employed by INS.

Some may wonder if creating a "New INS" with old ICE/ERO officers will accomplish the goals of reforming ICE. But this is not just rebranding. Separating ERO away from HSI will prevent DHS from blurring the line between civil law enforcement and criminal law enforcement. This will prevent HSI officers from being pulled off of vital criminal investigations to participate in civil immigration operations. In addition, the reality is that we must have civil immigration law enforcement, and ICE/ERO officers who first went on duty prior to January 20, 2025, are the best candidates we have for that job.

Professionalism

We can make immigration law enforcement conform to what we expect from other law enforcement agencies. Immigration enforcement officers should have training similar to other law enforcement officers. Starting in 2025, immigration enforcement officers began to receive only 47 days of training… and did not include Constitutional rules. Cutting law enforcement training to just 47 days and omitting training about the Constitutional foundations of law enforcement undermines the integrity of the agency.

As any newly minted naturalized U.S. citizen knows, the Constitution is "The Supreme Law of the Land." So it's only natural that we should expect our immigration law enforcement officers to actually know the Constitution and how it applies to civil immigration law enforcement. For example, they should know that the Fourth Amendment protects everyone in the United States, citizens and noncitizens alike, from unreasonable searches and seizures. They should also know that everyone inside the United States, regardless of their immigration status, is entitled to due process under the Fifth Amendment. Immigration enforcement officers' conduct as government officers must be in line with the Constitution. The only way to make sure this happens is to give them proper training before they start interacting with the public, and to hold them accountable if they violate this training.

Also, under any new immigration law, all immigration enforcement officers should be required to adhere to new rules to foster public trust. First of all, immigration enforcement officers should not wear masks to conceal their own identity. To protect them and their families, we need to have a new anti-doxxing law, but being able to see the faces of immigration enforcement officers is fundamental to public trust. In addition, we need to require that immigration enforcement officers wear visible identification and body-worn cameras.

ICE agents need to show their faces; this is a public safety issue. We have to be able to trust ICE agents. That begins with knowing their identity. Being able to see their faces and know their identity makes them accountable for their actions. For example, if an ICE officer needlessly pepper sprays someone in the face or shoots them, it is vitally important to know the officer's identity. If an ICE officer conceals his identity, it is difficult to hold him accountable for his actions.

Senator Padilla has already introduced a bill that would accomplish these things, called the VISIBLE Act. This is a common-sense approach, that has built-in protections for the officers, too, such as the ability to wear masks if their safety truly is an issue. But in most cases, this law would require them to show their faces and have their badge visible so we can know who they are, and so that we can trust them.

If you observe someone being arrested by an ICE officer, you should be able to have trust that the arrest is lawful. If you're an ICE officer, you should want to look professional and trustworthy. You shouldn't want to be confused with an outlaw. There's nothing impressive about an ICE agent looking like the bad guy from a train robbery in the wild west. Give ICE agents distinctive uniforms, similar to Border Patrol or to the old INS uniforms. And their vehicles should also clearly identify them, just like other law enforcement, so that people know who they're dealing with. Unmarked black SUVs do not inspire trust.

If an immigration agent is going to take away someone's liberty, even if the person is not in the country legally, the immigration agent should display their authority to do it as an agent of the United States government.

Agents should be required to display identification that includes what agency they work for and their name and badge number. Agents should not be allowed to conceal this with whatever tactical gear or clothing they might be wearing. If a U.S. citizen is videotaping an immigration agent's law enforcement actions (as they are permitted to do under the First Amendment), it should be apparent who the officer is.

It's important for agents to understand that covering their faces is not making them safer. They may feel that way because they don't want to be doxed, but in reality they look dangerous, unaccountable, and anonymous. Other law enforcement identify themselves and immigration enforcement agents need to do the same. Police face less danger by being more transparent because people know who they are. There's trust.

Moreover, ICE officers should take pride in their work, which means displaying who they are, and not hiding behind a mask for shame of what they're doing to people.

Anti-Doxxing

We should be concerned with the safety and well-being of law enforcement personnel. If we are going to mandate that immigration law enforcement officers show their faces to the world, we must also protect those officers and their families from abuse.

There is already an anti-doxxing statute under current federal law. 18 U.S.C. Section 119 makes it a crime for a person to knowingly publicly disclose restricted personal information about an immigration law enforcement officer or his or her immediate family member, if it's done "with the intent to threaten, intimidate, or incite the commission of a crime of violence" against the officer or family member (or "with the intent and knowledge" that the restricted personal information "will be used to threaten, intimidate, or facilitate the commission of a crime of violence" against the officer or family member).

Several states have enacted their own anti-doxxing type of laws to give law enforcement officers and others even more protection than the existing federal law. It might be surprising to some people that states where immigration officers have been infamously wearing masks, such as California, Oregon, Illinois, and Minnesota, already have strong anti-doxxing laws that give officers more protection than the existing federal law. But what is needed is a uniform anti-doxxing law that will protect immigration officers and their families throughout the United States.

One existing legislative proposal for a new federal anti-doxxing law is a bipartisan bill in Congress called the "Stop the Doxx Act" which would increase criminal penalties for doxxing. We certainly should want to deter doxxing, and increased criminal penalties could be helpful.

But in addition to stiffer criminal penalties for an offender, though, we could give practical relief to a doxxed officer. For example, the State of Washington has an anti-doxxing law (RCW 4.24.792) that has a provision to give a doxxed officer a civil cause of action against the person doing the doxxing. The Washington law allows an officer to recover compensatory and punitive damages, plus attorney's fees and emergency injunctive relief. It also allows a court to issue a temporary restraining order or injunction to stop the publication or disclosure of the officer's personal information. This is important because under the existing federal law, there is not currently a provision for a doxxed officer to have a court step in and order that the personal information be taken down from the internet.

Federal law could also go farther to prevent harm. The current federal law 18 U.S.C. Section 119 only makes it a crime to doxx an officer with the intent to threaten, intimidate, or incite a crime of violence. It might be difficult to prove intent, and it does not cover serious life disruptions that don't rise to a crime of violence. To remedy this, we could borrow further from the Washington law, which includes conduct done with "reckless disregard" for the risk that the publication of personal information will be used to harm the officer or his family. This would eliminate the difficulty of proving intent in order to hold the doxxer accountable. In addition, a new federal anti-doxxing law should protect against more harms than just a potential crime of violence. For example, the Washington law protects against publication of personal information that causes several different types of harm: any physical injury, significant economic injury, mental anguish, fear of serious bodily injury or death to the officer or family member, or a substantial life disruption.

One of the beauties of the Washington law is that it covers not just federal law enforcement officers, but also any individual. The protection goes both ways.

The Washington law also balances the need to protect people's personal information with the need to protect Constitutional rights of freedom of speech and the press. So, even under the enhanced anti-doxxing protections in the State of Washington, people can still call out a particular officer to criticize or identify them, just not in a way that publishes private information that is likely to create harm, fear, harassment, or serious disruption of the officer's life.

Therefore, I would propose that we should have a new federal anti-doxxing law that borrows heavily from the State of Washington's RCW 4.24.792 to accomplish these goals.

Priority Immigration Law Enforcement

We need a new standard system of immigration law enforcement that pairs local police with federal immigration agents to mandate that local police cooperate with ICE in a sensible way that keeps dangerous criminal immigrants off the streets to protect the public, and that is also reasonable. We need to have uniformity across the states regarding immigration detainers of immigrants who have been convicted of felonies.

Let's talk about what the new Priority Immigration Law Enforcement system would look like. This would be a uniform federal immigration law enforcement system that provides a safe and efficient way for federal immigration agents to take custody of noncitizens who are convicted of serious crimes before they get released. This new system would continue to rely on immigration agents being able to screen people using fingerprints when someone is booked into jail anywhere in the country. This helps the federal government know if someone is a noncitizen and if the person is being accused of a serious crime that would make their deportation a priority (if convicted). Then, the federal government can track the case and know if the person gets convicted of a deportable offense.

If there's a conviction for an aggravated felony, violent crime, drug trafficking, firearms, domestic violence, child abuse, sexual abuse, human trafficking, terrorism, or serious repeat offense, then this new Priority Enforcement system would require local jails to give federal immigration agents advance notice that the person is scheduled for release so that the immigration agents can show up and take custody when the person is released. The benefit of this type of Priority Enforcement system is that it allows immigration agents to focus on noncitizens who have been convicted of serious crimes. It avoids noncitizens getting caught in the net for traffic stops or less serious minor charges that may result in dropped charges or an acquittal. Also, by focusing on convictions, it recognizes that people are innocent until proven guilty and it avoids the problem of the federal government being responsible for pretrial detention and for transporting noncitizens from a federal immigration detention center to a local city or county courthouse for their trial.

This would also serve to preserve community trust in police law enforcement because it would not rely on local police to question people about their immigration status. We do not want to discourage crime victims or witnesses from talking to the police out of fear that the police might arrest them for their immigration status. In jails, local police involvement would be limited to confirming a person's identity, letting the federal government know when their scheduled release is, and then facilitating custody transfer after conviction. This Priority Enforcement system would also provide that the federal government would reimburse local governments for any local expenditures that result from participation.

This new Priority Immigration Law Enforcement system would eliminate the conflict between the federal and local governments over immigration law enforcement cooperation because it (1) creates a uniform national system with clear rules to ensure public safety, (2) makes sure that the "worst of the worst" really are taken into custody by immigration agents, and (3) does not drag people into it if they pose no threat to society.

In order to make room for the new Priority Immigration Law Enforcement system, the first thing we would do is to repeal Section 287(g), which puts noncitizens in the hands of local law enforcement, even without having committed any crime. The 287(g) program was put into place in the 1996 IIRIRA law. 287(g) has a few major problems. One problem is that it's a voluntary system that states and cities can either opt into or decide not to participate in, which has created a patchwork of immigration law enforcement that currently depends on the state, county, or city to determine what level of cooperation (if any) there is with federal agents. The second problem is that 287(g) is over-broad in who it sweeps in, which makes it unpopular with many local police departments who want to balance public safety with community trust in law enforcement.

Here's an example of why the current 287(g) program is too broad. Currently, in a place such as Phoenix where there is a 287(g) agreement in place, for noncitizens who get arrested by the police for a minor offense, if they post a bond, then instead of being released to the street to go home, they get picked up by ICE at the jail. (Also, if the case gets dropped right after the arrest, which happens sometimes, then the person gets picked up by ICE instead of being let go). ICE holds noncitizens in detention and ICE usually refuses to transport them back to the criminal court for their hearings or trial, so they get a warrant out for them. The state does not get to finish its prosecution, and the immigrant does not get to defend himself. This is why many of the ICE reports of immigrant detentions say that the noncitizen has "charges pending." ICE is interfering with the administration of justice by arresting people who are awaiting trial and oftentimes not letting them go to criminal court. Or, in some localities, the police don't even bother to book the person on the minor charges they were arrested for; instead, the police can just hand them off to ICE.

Another thing that 287(g) does is that it creates "287(g) task forces," made up of local police officers. If you want to "follow the money," I would highly recommend reading the excellent article by Ken Klippenstein referenced in the Sources at the back of this book. According to Mr. Klippenstein's reporting, the 287(g) task forces are created by agreements between DHS and local law enforcement agencies, whereby DHS deputizes police officers to participate in civil immigration law enforcement. Local police agencies can then choose to have deputized officers identify noncitizens without lawful immigration status by interrogating both drivers and passengers present in vehicles during traffic stops regarding their immigration status. With this power, the police officers can detain drivers or passengers and transfer them to ICE for being unlawfully present in the United States even if they have not committed a crime. DHS touts this as being a "force multiplier." For police departments, it lets them get in on the action financially because, under 287(g), DHS reimburses the local police departments for the cost of officer salaries and vehicles, with added financial incentives for arrests. The effect of this is that local police can make a traffic stop for a truck carrying workers, and then detain the occupants for civil immigration violations, and get paid to do it.

287(g) task forces might be an efficient way for DHS to catch more undocumented immigrants who have not been convicted of crimes, but by doing so it needlessly separates U.S. citizen children from their parents facing deportation, ends up costing the United States government a great deal of money, and stops those workers from contributing to the economy by doing their jobs.

If we eliminate 287(g) and implement a nationwide Priority Immigration Law Enforcement system for immigrants who actually have criminal convictions, we can catch all of the immigrants who have proven themselves to be dangerous and, at the same time, not haphazardly arrest any peaceful undocumented immigrant who comes into contact with law enforcement.

Accountability

Under the current law, there are a number of legal roadblocks that protect federal officers from being held accountable for using excessive force, even killing someone, such as Renee Good or Alex Pretti.

If we intend to deter immigration agents from using excessive force, we must give them a consequence for doing it. There is currently a bill in Congress called the Qualified Immunity Abolition Act of 2026 which, if passed into law, would allow a victim to sue federal law enforcement officers such as ICE officers for using excessive force while acting under color of federal law (in other words, if they unnecessarily shoot someone while acting as an ICE agent). This bill would eliminate the current defense of "qualified immunity" by an officer saying that he thought what he was doing was right.

The future of immigration law enforcement

If we enact the ideas in this chapter to reform ICE, we can make immigration law enforcement something that Americans can widely support again. Part of coming together as a country to solve the immigration crisis is to have a reasonable plan for immigration law enforcement. Re-creating INS, along with the other proposals above, would be the foundation. The next chapter is a set of proposed new rules for how immigration law enforcement can be civil again.

CHAPTER 12

New Rules for Civil Immigration Law Enforcement

New Rule No. 1: Be Civil

We need to have new rules regarding the enforcement of immigration laws in the interior of the United States to ensure that people's Constitutional rights are protected. Since 2025, we have seen an increase in immigration law enforcement actions in the "interior" of the United States: in cities far away from the border, such as Los Angeles, Chicago, and Minneapolis. For example, in early June 2025, the government began immigration enforcement raids in and around the Los Angeles area, including the counties of Los Angeles, Ventura, Santa Barbara, San Luis Obispo, Orange, Riverside, and San Bernardino. The government called this "Operation At Large," and it involved roving patrols of armed and masked immigration agents at local car washes, Home Depots, tow yards, bus stops, farms, recycling centers, churches, and parks. According to court records, immigration agents stopped Latino U.S. citizens and questioned them regarding their citizenship and agents demanded that U.S. citizens provide proof of their U.S. citizenship.

Let's take a moment to examine what gives immigration officers the power to stop people and demand proof of immigration status. What are the limitations, and how do we make sure that these stops comply with the Fourth Amendment?

The power of immigration officers to interrogate people about their immigration status comes from Immigration and Nationality Act Section 287, which is codified at 8 United States Code Section 1357. Under that law, immigration officers are authorized "to interrogate any alien or person believed to be an alien as to his right to be or to remain in the United States." (But this statutory provision under Section 287(a)(1) does not relieve them of their Constitutional duties.)

This is where they get their power to stop people all over the United States. It allows an immigration officer to stop people who he or she believes might be an "alien" and interrogate them, asking them things like, "Where were you born?" This law allows them to interrogate people without a warrant. This is why they think they can just stop people in the street or pull people over in their cars and demand to see their I.D. and demand to know where they were born.

What is an "alien"? Under the Immigration and Nationality Act, "The term 'alien' means any person not a citizen or national of the United States." INA Section 101(a)(3). (By the way, a "national of the United States" is either a U.S. citizen or a noncitizen from a place such as American Samoa or Swains Island (U.S. possessions) who owe allegiance to the U.S.)

Under the code of federal regulations, immigration officers "may briefly detain" a person for questioning if the officers have "a reasonable suspicion, based on specific articulable facts, that the person being questioned... is an alien illegally in the United States." 8 C.F.R. Section 287.8(b)(2)

In *U.S. v. Brignoni-Ponce*, the Supreme Court ruled that immigration officers may stop an individual "only if they are aware of specific articulable facts, together with rational inferences from those facts, that reasonably warrant suspicion" that the person might be illegally in the country. After *Brignoni-Ponce*, federal courts have held that this requires more than just a general suspicion or a hunch. Also, courts have held that a government official cannot form "reasonable suspicion" based on things like Mexican ancestry because undocumented immigrants are not the only ones who might have physical characteristics that make them appear to have Mexican ancestry. Many native-born and naturalized U.S. citizens also have Mexican ancestry, so "looking Mexican" has nothing to do with whether or not a person might be undocumented.

Theoretically, the law does not give immigration officers completely unfettered discretion to stop anyone and interrogate them about whether they might be an "alien illegally in the United States" A person being stopped is protected by the Fourth Amendment right to be free of unreasonable searches and seizures and the Fifth Amendment right to due process.

The Fourth Amendment protects everyone in the United States from unreasonable searches and seizures by government officials, regardless of the person's immigration status. The Fourth Amendment obviously applies to U.S. citizens, but it also protects anyone else who is physically in the U.S., such as lawful permanent residents, non-immigrant visa holders, and even undocumented immigrants. If a DHS agent tackles someone, that's obviously a "seizure." But so is stopping someone and demanding their identification, even if physical force is not used against the person. The Fourth Amendment is supposed to prevent government officials from arbitrarily interfering with people's privacy and personal security. In other words, the Fourth Amendment is supposed to prevent immigration officials from stopping someone and restraining their freedoms, unless the officer has reason to believe that the person is in the United States illegally.

In the case of the Los Angeles area roving patrols, the government relied solely on just four factors to come up with reasonable suspicion to believe that people were "aliens illegally in the U.S." The government attempted to justify their "reasonable suspicion" by saying that they thought someone's race or ethnicity, speaking Spanish (or English with an accent), doing manual labor, and being at places like bus stops, car washes or day laborer locations (or some combination of those things) indicated a likelihood of being in the U.S. illegally. The ACLU filed a lawsuit in federal district court against the Department of Homeland Security because these things constitute racial profiling and are not actual indicators that someone is unlawfully in the U.S. The case is called *Vasquez Perdomo v. Noem.* The lawsuit alleged that the government has a policy, pattern, and practice of stopping people without reasonable suspicion that the person is within the United States illegally, and that the government's policy, pattern, and practice violated the Fourth Amendment of the U.S. Constitution.

In the federal district court, the court granted a Temporary Restraining Order (TRO) against the government, prohibiting them from using just those four factors as the basis for "reasonable suspicion" that a person is in the U.S. illegally. The Court reasoned that using just these four factors as the basis for thinking that a person is in the U.S. illegally amounts to racial profiling because these things are also common for people who are in the U.S. legally. In other words, the federal district court said that these four factors, by themselves, do not mean that a person might be in the U.S. without authorization. The Court cited evidence that nearly half of the population of the Los Angeles area is made up of people who identify as Latino, and over a third of that population speaks Spanish.

The government asked the Ninth Circuit to pause the TRO, and the Ninth Circuit denied the government's motion (except for one small part of the TRO, where the TRO had said "except as permitted by law" which the Ninth Circuit agreed was vague). The Ninth Circuit agreed with the district court that the government racially profiled people as a basis for "reasonable suspicion" of illegal immigration status.

The government appealed to the U.S. Supreme Court, where the case is known as *Noem v. Vasquez Perdomo*. At the Supreme Court, Justice Kavanaugh stated that the government *is* allowed to use just these four factors by themselves to have "reasonable suspicion" that a person is an alien in the U.S. illegally. According to Justice Kavanaugh, immigration agents are merely conducting "brief stops for questioning," that take only a minute, and that U.S. citizens and others in the U.S. legally are free to go as soon as they show they are legally in the U.S. However, there are three big problems with this analysis:

First, these four factors are not proof of illegal presence in the U.S. For example, 47 percent of population in the Los Angeles area identifies as Hispanic or Latino. And over 37 percent of the population of Los Angeles County speaks Spanish at home. For example, if a person appears to be Hispanic, works at a car wash, and speaks Spanish in Los Angeles, that person is not more likely to be a noncitizen illegally in the U.S. just based on those facts. This is a stereotype and there's no evidence that it's true.

Second, it imposes a burden on everyone in the United States to carry proof of their U.S. citizenship or legal immigration status, in case they are ever stopped by immigration officers.

Third, the reality is that immigration officers do not just "let people go" as Justice Kavanaugh posits. Instead, there have been many documented cases where U.S. citizens are arrested and detained for hours before immigration officers verify their citizenship and finally release them. Not only that, but the immigration officers use force to stop people, resulting in injuries. If a person is a U.S. citizen walking around or working, there is no reason that they should be subject to being seized by immigration officers based on nothing more than being Hispanic and speaking Spanish. As Justice Sotomayor stated in her dissent, "Countless people in the Los Angeles area have been grabbed, thrown to the ground, and handcuffed simply because of their looks, their accents, and the fact they make a living by doing manual labor."

Although the Fourth Amendment is supposed to protect every person's constitutional right to be free from arbitrary interference by law enforcement officers, this right has been severely eroded by Justice Kavanaugh's opinion because it allows immigration officers to stop people because of how they look, how they speak, and if they work in a low-paying job. The result is that all over the United States immigration officials can racially profile people to detain them based on things that, in fact, have little or nothing to do with whether they might be in the United States illegally. This is the current state of the law in the U.S.

In January 2026, the Brooklyn Park, Minnesota, police chief spoke at a news conference at the Minnesota State Capitol, with other Minnesota police chiefs in attendance. He said that he has had a good relationship in the past with ICE officers. But he said that recently, several of his police officers who are "people of color," as he said, have been stopped by ICE while the police officers were off-duty driving their vehicles. The ICE officers interrogated off-duty police officers about where they were born, their immigration status, and whether or not they could prove that they're a U.S. citizen. We have a high regard for police officers so we assume that the off-duty police officers were not doing anything wrong to justify being stopped. They were stopped for no reason other than the color of their skin. The ICE officers obviously thought the law, as interpreted by the Supreme Court, authorizes these Kavanaugh-stops.

We could change the law to require that immigration officers have probable cause (instead of just "reasonable suspicion") to believe that a person is in the U.S. illegally in order to stop the person, and that race, ethnicity, language, location, and type of work by themselves cannot be the reason for believing the person is a noncitizen illegally in the U.S. This would be a higher standard. If we did this, then for an immigration officer to stop someone, the officer would need to already know specific information about the particular person to justify a belief that they are in the U.S. illegally. If we require that immigration officers have probable cause that a person is in the U.S. illegally, and can't use just those four factors by themselves, it would prevent them from racial profiling as the basis for immigration stops.

Will requiring probable cause, instead of just "reasonable suspicion," of unlawful presence, make immigration officers' jobs more difficult? What will happen if we require that immigration agents know something specific about a person in order to form the belief that the person is an "alien illegally in the U.S."? The answer is that they will have to have a really good reason to stop someone. If they have a good reason to believe that a particular person is probably in the U.S. illegally (not just based on a stereotype), then they can still stop them. But they won't be able to racially profile any more based simply on the combination of person's race or ethnicity, speaking Spanish (or English with an accent), presence at a particular location, or type of work. In cities around the country, this is the expectation that Americans have for how immigration officers should treat them: No stopping people without probable cause based on relevant facts (not stereotypes) to believe that a person is unlawfully present in the U.S. And let's stop using the word "alien" to describe a noncitizen.

What About the Border?

For the sake of argument, let's say that it might make sense to give immigration officers broad power to stop people and interrogate them about their immigration status near the border, based on "reasonable suspicion" of unlawful presence. The importance of border security is paramount, and we're not trying to erode border security. We don't need to change how the Border Patrol decides who to question, detain, or arrest when they are near the border and keeping the border secure. On the border, the rules can be a little bit looser, allowing Border Patrol officers to stop people based on "reasonable suspicion" that the person is from another country and is in the United States illegally.

But what makes sense for the border doesn't necessarily make sense for everywhere else in the country. Applying these current tactics all over the United States harms U.S. citizens who get caught up in the dragnet. People who live in the interior of the United States do not want their neighborhoods patrolled by the Border Patrol or ICE and to be treated like their Constitutionally protected rights can be diminished under the guise of the immigration law. The Border Patrol and ICE should not be operating in the interior of the United States in cities like Los Angeles, Chicago, New York, and Minneapolis, as if they're on the border. Taken to the extreme, these tactics could be used for the purpose of intimidating U.S. citizens, resulting in the manifestation of Mr. Feingold's legitimate concerns.

The 50-Mile Rule

First, we need to decide on where the law changes from the "Wild West" on the border to civilization in the cities of America. I would suggest 50 miles as the "Border Enforcement Area."

Fifty miles is plenty of room for Border Patrol to do everything they need to do to keep the border secure. We don't want to unnecessarily restrict immigration officers from doing their jobs near the border and at the airport or ports when they are making sure people coming in to the U.S. have the right documents. But if an immigration agent is at least 50 miles from the border, we need new rules regarding immigration officers' power to interrogate people. More than 50 miles away from the land border, an immigration officer should not be allowed to stop a person and interrogate them regarding their immigration status unless the officer has probable cause, based on information known about that specific person, that he or she is in the U.S. illegally.

If we limit "reasonable suspicion" "Kavanaugh stops" to within 50 miles of the border, we are still giving Border Patrol officers the same tool they have always had to patrol the border and stop suspicious people who might be in the U.S. illegally. But we need to change the law so that immigration agents cannot use this tool against U.S. citizens or anybody else within the interior of the United States, more than 50 miles from the border.

There will be some readers concerned that Kavanaugh stops shouldn't even be allowed within 50 miles of the border. While that is a valid concern, it is unclear how we might remedy this without the counter-claim that it would prevent Border Patrol from doing its actual job of patrolling the border.

You might be thinking, "What's the big deal? If an ICE officer stops me, I'll just tell them that I'm a U.S citizen, born and raised here, and then go on my way." Yes, but the point is that nobody should be stopping you or anyone else, asking "Where were you born?" solely based upon the color of your skin, the language you speak or how you speak it, the type of work you do, or which location you're at. That's just wrong. Stereotypes are not a reason to think that a person is from another country and is in the U.S. illegally. If your answer to these real-life scenarios is, "Oh, well, they found people who weren't supposed to be here, so that's fine," you're missing the point. The point is that the Fourth Amendment prohibits the government from making unreasonable searches and seizures, and Kavanaugh stops are not objectively reasonable.

To accomplish this, we should add a new rule to amend Section 287 of the Immigration and Nationality Act (8 U.S.C. 1357) :

> **"50 MILE RULE FOR IMMIGRATION STOPS**
> (1) PROHIBITION. An Immigration officer is not allowed to stop a person more than 50 miles from the border, unless the officer has probable cause based on specific personal information (not just things such as race, ethnicity, language, work, or location) that the person is illegally in the United States.
>
> (2) EXCLUSION. If an Immigration officer violates subparagraph (1) above, then an Immigration Judge must throw out any statement, evidence, or information obtained as a direct or indirect result of the stop. (In other words, if an immigration officer breaks the law and stops somebody without probable cause of unlawful presence, the government can't use anything against them if they discovered it because of the illegal stop.)
>
> (3) CIVIL REMEDY. Any person subjected to a stop in violation of this subsection can sue any officer or officers who participated in the stop, and they are liable for damages and attorney fees."

This simple change would eliminate the loose interpretation of "reasonable suspicion" of being in the U.S. without authorization that ICE officers currently use to detain almost anyone, including U.S. citizens.

Let's make immigration officers respectable again. Serious ICE reform is in order. We are a nation of laws. Let's have a law that tells ICE how to act and how to treat people. This will be the law that ICE officers are taught in training and the law they will follow. As it is, we give ICE officers the authority to stop and detain people for interrogation, which can result in a person (even a U.S. citizen) being "detained" in a jail-like locked facility that looks a lot like prison. Immigration officers have serious power against people. They need very clear instructions about what they can and cannot do, because right now there's too much room for ICE officers to abuse their power. This is not about whether we let them enforce the law. This is about *how* they enforce the law. We should not tolerate them brutalizing communities.

If we do this, a lot of our problems with ICE will be solved. ICE can still get the criminals and people crossing the border illegally, but they won't be able to stop people on the street or in their vehicles in cities across the United States based on racial profiling.

Judicial Warrants Should Be Required for Civil Arrests and Home Entries

For arrests and home entries, we need a new rule that is simple and easy to understand, that clearly lays out the procedure to arrest someone in the interior of the United States for an immigration violation, and requires that a real judge sign off on it. That way, the public can trust that it is the administration of justice and not injustice. This is what's required to regain public trust.

Right now, an ICE officer can arrest a person without a warrant if the officer has "reason to believe" the person is unlawfully present in the United States and "is likely to escape before a warrant can be obtained." But when is a person "likely to escape"? An ICE officer would probably say, "When is a person *not* likely to escape?" ICE officers think people are always likely to escape, unless they're trapped in an ICE office.

We should change the law and make it more like the law that applies to police. Let's make it so that an immigration officer can arrest a person if the officer has probable cause that the person is deportable for a criminal conviction and the officer has a warrant issued by a judge. This would make it more like arrests by the police.

Here's what I propose should be the new bright-line rule for making civil immigration arrests in the interior of the United States: ICE can arrest any deportable non-U.S. citizen who is at least 50 miles from the border only pursuant to a judicial arrest warrant based on probable cause that the person has been convicted of a crime that makes them inadmissible or deportable from the United States. Officers can still "do their job." If ICE discovers that a person is unlawfully present in the United States and has been convicted of a serious crime, they can arrest them. That's fine. But get a warrant signed by a United States magistrate judge saying that the judge has found there's probable cause that a particular person is not a citizen or national of the United States and that the person is deportable from the United States under either Section 212 or 237 of Immigration and Nationality Act. This does not change who can be deported. This just makes it more orderly. If ICE identifies a person who is deportable for a criminal conviction, they can get an arrest warrant any time of day or night from a U.S. magistrate judge. Judges are already used to doing this.

Notice to Appear System

Deportation is a civil matter. In other types of civil court cases, the plaintiff files a complaint with the appropriate court and serves the complaint on the defendant. For a noncitizen who has not been convicted of a crime, this does not require an arrest or detention. So, how will immigration officers make people go to court? In immigration court, instead of there being a complaint, there is already a document called the "Notice to Appear" which is written by an immigration officer and given to the immigrant who the government wants to deport. The Notice to Appear is like a cross between a criminal complaint and a traffic ticket. If an immigration officer discovers someone who is in the United States without legal authorization, all the officer has to do is write up a Notice to Appear and serve it on the person, and then the person is legally obligated to appear in court at the time and place written on the Notice to Appear. An immigration officer can give a person a Notice to Appear to go to immigration court, just like a police officer writes a ticket. We already have this in the immigration laws. This is how civil legal proceedings are conducted: by giving the person notice of the allegations and legal charges against them and then demanding that they answer in court. If the person does not appear for immigration court, then the judge can issue a warrant for their arrest. If an immigration officer serves an immigrant with a Notice to Appear in immigration court, there is no need to also arrest them if they are not dangerous to the community.

Warrants for Home Entries

In 2026, there has been a controversy over whether ICE can enter someone's private property without a warrant. In the United States, everyone, including immigrants, has an expectation of privacy in their home. The Fourth Amendment guarantees that people in the United States will be free from unreasonable searches and seizures by the government. Most people, including judges, agree that ICE does not have the legal authority under the current law to enter someone's home without a warrant. Up until recently in 2026, not even ICE made the argument that they could enter someone's home without a judicial warrant. But in 2026, it became public that ICE had a secret memo stating that immigration officers could enter a home without a judicial warrant. All that was needed, they said, was an administrative warrant signed by an ICE officer. By mid-February, 2026, DHS officials began to publicly defend this policy.

We need to make it clear in the immigration laws that the only way an immigration officer can enter someone's home is either (1) with a judicial warrant or (2) by written consent corroborated by video of the person giving consent. This is basically what the Fourth Amendment already guarantees, but we need to make it crystal clear that a judicial warrant is required to enter a person's home without their consent, and what kind of evidence of consent we expect to see if an officer says the entry was consensual.

How do we make sure ICE doesn't just ignore the law and do it anyway? Make another "suppression" rule. If ICE violates these laws and arrests a person without probable cause and a warrant, then whatever evidence they obtain, such as an admission, should be inadmissible in court.

If we make the above changes to the immigration law, then Immigration officers such as ICE agents can still "do their job" to enforce the law. But these changes will make it more orderly, transparent, trustworthy... and legal.

New Rule No. 2: Stay Out of Schools, Churches, and Hospitals

Most Americans agree that ICE should not be arresting immigrants in certain places of safety. In a national survey by Pew Research, over 60% of Americans agree that ICE should not make immigration arrests in places of worship, schools, or hospitals.

Since January 20, 2025, there have been at least forty-nine ICE enforcement actions that took place either at or very close to schools, which was terrifying for the children who were present. ICE has arrested people at or near places of worship at least eight times. And there have been at least nine ICE enforcement operations at hospitals or other medical facilities.

In January 2026, ICE acted like a patient at a hospital in Minneapolis was "under arrest." It was reported that on December 31, 2025, a person went to the Emergency Room of Hennepin County Medical Center in Minneapolis, Minnesota. ICE went in after him and sat with him and "kept him company" for over 24 hours. They did not present an arrest warrant or any authority that they should be there. The person apparently needed extended medical care. ICE stayed with him for over 24 hours. But what were the ICE officers there to do? Apparently, they intended to take him into custody. They sure kept an eye on him. They went into his room and handcuffed him to the bed, even, and ICE denied visitation to the person's family. Two officers at a time sat by his bed, rotating every four hours.

So he must have been a criminal, right? That's how you would expect the police to treat a criminal. But the police were not there. And this person did not get transported from a jail or a prison. The person went to the ER on their own. It was just ICE inserting itself in a hospital, guarding a person, making sure he did not leave on his own, making sure no family or friends visited him, and generally just keeping him in their custody. In other words, ICE was trying to arrest him while he was getting medical treatment.

If the police weren't trying to arrest the person, then why does ICE need to be there? ICE spokespeople always act like everybody should be their "partner" and do their part to make ICE's job of arresting people easier. But inside a hospital?

If a person is receiving medical care at a hospital, things are bad enough for them. They've already had a pretty bad day. They don't need an ICE officer to stand guard over them while doctors and nurses try to help them. Can you imagine the stress of being in a hospital bed and being under the constant surveillance of an ICE officer inside your hospital room? You would probably be worried that they would arrest you, hold you without bond, and then try to deport you. . . because that's exactly what their intent was. So, you wouldn't be able to relax and try to recover. And imagine being in a hospital and also worrying about your own family members, and whether or not they might get arrested by ICE.

It would also cause tension for other patients in the hospital receiving medical treatment, and for the medical staff. Knowing that ICE might be in the hospital at all might cause some people to just decide to not go to the hospital, even if they really needed to. We don't want to discourage people from seeking medical treatment because they're afraid they might get arrested by ICE.

By the way, we're not talking about changing the rules for police. We're only talking about how ICE conducts civil immigration law enforcement. The police can still do whatever they need to do under the law. After all, they are law enforcement officers, whose mission is to protect and serve the public. We support the police.

We should make a rule that ICE is not allowed to arrest people at hospitals. And the same thing should go for schools and churches. If there is a person who ICE has the authority to arrest and that person goes into a hospital, school, or church, the rule needs to be that ICE has to wait until they come out to arrest them. This is not saying ICE can't do their job. They just can't take their job into these places, because we, as a society, think that hospitals, schools, and churches are safe spaces where the inherent objective of being there outweighs the need for ICE to arrest the person. All we're saying is, it can wait. In addition to just being more humane, this rule would help Americans. It would reduce the possibility that a U.S. citizen might erroneously be arrested by ICE. Most of us can agree that the last thing we want is for ICE to arrest U.S. citizens.

Having this new rule would also make it so people wouldn't be afraid to go to school, the hospital, or their place of worship, for fear of getting arrested by ICE. We are the United States of

America. No one should be staying home from school out of fear of ICE.

CHAPTER 13

Stop Locking People Up for Fun and Profit

"We have to look for ways of treating people humanely, treating people with the dignity that they have."

—*Pope Leo XIV*

IN THE UNITED STATES OVER the past 30 years, unfortunately we as a society have become accustomed to the idea that there is a legitimacy to at least the idea, or premise, of immigration jails. We have assumed that there was a legitimate reason to have immigration detention centers in the first place. But beginning in 2025, there has also been a widespread questioning of these assumptions, as Americans have begun to see we have been sold a lie that the people ICE is locking up are dangerous.

As a nation, we need to reconsider whether "detaining" (incarcerating) approximately 70,000 immigrants per day for the purpose of deportation is right. The fact is, at least 70% of the immigrants who are incarcerated in immigration jails have no criminal record whatsoever. Only a very small percentage of the incarcerated immigrants, approximately 5% or less, have been convicted of a violent crime. We need to ask ourselves why we are doing this.

What purpose is it serving? Is it for some legitimate purpose? Or is it meant simply to punish immigrants and provide a payday of billions of dollars for private prison companies at the expense of U.S. taxpayers?

This is not the first time in our nation's history that the government has locked up a large group of people based on flimsy justifications. During World War II, the U.S. government forcibly removed approximately 120,000 people of Japanese ancestry from their homes and locked them up in internment camps. The majority (approximately 80,000) were U.S. citizens who were born in the United States. They were as American as anybody. The rest (approximately 40,000) were long-term immigrant residents of the United States who had been born in Japan and legally immigrated here, but who were barred from becoming U.S. citizens under the immigration laws that existed at that time.

The mass incarceration of Japanese Americans and Japanese immigrants was authorized by Executive Order 9066 signed by President Franklin D. Roosevelt in 1942, in response to the attack on Pearl Harbor. When the nation of Japan attacked Pearl Harbor on December 7, 1941, it was a devastating blow to the United States. It was truly a day that lives in infamy, and it changed the course of history. It created widespread panic in the American public, throughout the United States. But looking back, the events of that day obviously were not a reflection on the 40,000 Japanese immigrants and 80,000 Japanese Americans who were living in the United States.

Within the U.S. government at the time, there was not agreement that mass incarceration was the right thing to do. A Naval Intelligence officer, Kenneth Ringle, wrote a report (known as The Ringle Report) which concluded that the Japanese Americans (U.S. citizens) were loyal to the United States and posed absolutely no risk to the United States. These were people who had been born in the United States to immigrant parents who loved the United States. They wanted to defend the U.S., not harm it.

Even the FBI Director, J. Edgar Hoover, was not in favor of mass internment. In February 1942, FBI Director Hoover sent a letter to the U.S. Attorney General Francis Biddle and wrote, "The necessity for mass evacuation is based primarily upon public and political pressure rather than factual data."

U.S. Attorney General Biddle agreed that the Japanese Americans should not be incarcerated, but did not stand in the way of internment camps. In his later memoir, he wrote, "At no time did we have any evidence that Japanese Americans were engaged in espionage or sabotage."

In 1980, Congress created the U.S. Commission on Wartime Relocation and Internment of Civilians to investigate the incarceration of Japanese Americans during World War II. The Commission found that the incarceration was not a result of military necessity. The Commission concluded that the mass incarceration resulted from "race prejudice, war hysteria, and a failure of political leadership."

We should learn from history about ourselves as Americans. In the current context of immigration detention, there are echoes today of racial prejudice, "criminal alien" hysteria, and political leadership not standing up for what's right in the face of political pressure from a small but vocal minority.

Some might object to this analogy and say I'm comparing apples and oranges. Someone might contrast the current immigration situation and argue that, even if the Japanese internment turned out to not be justified, the immigrants being detained today are in the United States illegally in the first place. Someone might argue that they broke the law by breaking the immigration laws, so they somehow don't have the same expectation of liberty.

These objections fail to consider the Constitutional protections that all people in the United States enjoy. The Fifth Amendment of the U.S. Constitution guarantees each person in the United States, even recent arrivals and even immigrants who once upon a time broke the law by coming here illegally, the right to not have their liberty taken away without due process. "Due process" means two things. First, there has to be a procedural process. Second, there has to be a reason to justify taking away someone's liberty. In today's immigration situation, the government is arresting many immigrants without there being an individual process to determine if they should be arrested or without a good reason to justify the incarceration (such as actual danger to the community).

Also, some immigrants who have been arrested are people who were brought here as children and have DACA (Deferred Action for Childhood Arrivals). DACA recipients are somewhat reminiscent of the Japanese Americans who were incarcerated during World War II because they pledge their allegiance to the United States but the United States government doesn't accept them. As of July 2026, the U.S. government is actively paving the way for their deportation by, on the one hand, slow-rolling their DACA renewals and, on the other, telling immigration judges that DACA by itself is not a reason to stop deportations.

There have been several reasons for the growth of immigration detention in the United States. The border crisis of 2021-2024 gave rise to some public opinion that immigrants who came to the U.S. during the recent border surge should be deported. In 2024, President Trump capitalized on this sentiment by running on the campaign of the "largest deportation machine in history." Also, there have been a handful of well-publicized murders committed by noncitizens. The government has used these outlier crimes by noncitizens to fuel hysteria over "criminal aliens," even though most of the immigrant arrests have been long-term undocumented immigrants without any criminal history at all and who just want to work and take care of their families, or are recently arrived asylum-seekers who are attempting to legally process their asylum requests. The idea that these people are "criminal aliens" is nothing more than propaganda, lies told about a group of people. Because the truth is that generally speaking noncitizens are just as peaceful as U.S. citizens, if not more so.

This propaganda has led to increased Congressional budgets for immigration detention, creating a multi-billion dollar market for private prison companies. For example, the 2025 One Big Beautiful Bill Act provided for approximately $45 billion to be paid by the federal government for immigration detention. In the June 2026 Secure America Act, Congress appropriated an additional $31 billion to ICE. According to the government's budget proposal, much of this money is to be used to expand immigration jail capacity for up to 100,000 single adults and up to 30,000 people in family detention.

The government should not be detaining immigrants who pose no threat to the safety of their community and who are likely to appear for their hearings at immigration court. The government always likes to say, "This is a civil matter," when they lock people up. They like to tout that it's civil and not criminal, so that the constitutional protections in criminal law don't apply. In reality, though, the effect of this civil vs. criminal detention distinction is that, on the one hand, a person who gets arrested by the police for a criminal offense gets to see a judge often within hours to ask to be released on bail, but a person arrested by ICE for a civil immigration violation might have to wait weeks or months to see a judge just to be told that he or she is subject to "mandatory detention" even with no criminal history.

The "civil" nature of immigration detention is also distorted by the very language used to describe it. For example, when ICE arrests someone, it is called "detaining them." But in reality, it's not a "detainer." Detaining someone implies that it's temporary in nature, and that it's something less than an arrest. But when ICE arrests someone and takes them into custody to be held in a jail called a "detention center," they call it "detaining them" because the immigration law uses that term "detain." Let's just call it what it is: an arrest and incarceration.

There should be a presumption that immigrants are not a danger to the community and should not be arrested unless there's a very good reason for it. If a noncitizen is undocumented and has never been convicted of a crime, there should also be presumption that the person will appear for court to answer the immigration charges. We don't need to lock the person up to ensure their appearance for a civil court proceeding. We need to make it so that immigration arrests are only for noncitizens who are at or near the border, or for noncitizens who have been convicted of a serious crime.

If an immigrant is not already in custody for a crime, meaning they're free on the street or at home, immigration officers should not be arresting them just to make them go to immigration court. We should stop wasting money on holding people in immigration jail while they have court. Immigration jail detention centers are prisons; the facility has to take care of the person instead of the person taking care of himself.

Why should we take an able-bodied, hard-working person away from his family and his job, where he was a fully productive person, and lock him up so taxpayers have to provide him a different place to live (inside an immigration jail) and we have to provide him with food and medical care? There's nothing about this that's better than just letting the person live at home with their family, go to their job and take care of their own medical care, and every couple months take a day off and go to immigration court until it's decided whether or not they get to stay in the United States.

If the person is held in immigration jail for three months, for example, the government is paying the prison company a huge sum of money to minimally feed, house, and care for that person, at great financial expense to the citizens of the United States. If the person has never been convicted of a crime, there's absolutely no justification for thinking the person is a danger to the community. The person is not dangerous. We don't need to be locking him or her up away from their family and away from their job.

Not only is immigration detention a waste of money for the U.S. government and American citizens, but it has also become a humanitarian blight on our country. The conditions in the detention centers are horrible and inhumane. Just in terms of physical space, human beings have basic needs that are not being met in immigration detention. In some cases, people are being locked in cages for days where there is so little space that they are sitting or standing shoulder to shoulder with no room to move about. For example, Congressman Jamie Raskin witnessed a room full of 55 men standing shoulder-to-shoulder in a small room. They were locked in this room for several days with no shower and no place to sleep other than the cold concrete floor.

Many people are speaking out against this. The conditions in immigration detention centers are worse than you would expect even from jails or prisons. We would expect that a civil detention center would provide basic things like physical space for detainees, edible food in sufficient amounts to provide basic sustenance, and medical care to ensure that immigrants are at least kept alive. You wouldn't expect people to be dying. But that's what has been happening.

There has been a sharp rise in the number of immigrant deaths in ICE detention. In 2025, there were at least 31 deaths in ICE custody, which made it the deadliest year for ICE in over 20 years. In the first 6 months of 2026, there have already been at least 20 individuals who have died in ICE custody. The deaths have resulted from such things as seizures, heart failure, respiratory failure, tuberculosis, suicide, and homicide. We should not be numb to these deaths. These deaths resulted from lack of care, not inevitability.

The Associated Press reported the case of Geraldo Lunas Campos. Mr. Lunas Campos died in a detention center in Texas in 2026. ICE stated that he died when they tried to save him from suicide. But a witness told the Associated Press that he was handcuffed and guards held him down while another guard put an arm around his neck and squeezed the life out of him. According to the Associated Press, the El Paso County Medical Examiner's Office issued a report that "determined the cause of death was asphyxia due to neck and torso compression."

There has been extensive reporting on the Camp East Montana detention center where Mr. Lunas Campos died. In July 2026, Human Rights Watch and the ACLU published a report based on interviews with 71 detainees. They reported many serious allegations of abuse, medical neglect, unsanitary conditions.

Let's Not Forget About Alligator Alcatraz

The only thing cool about Alligator Alcatraz was the alliteration. The nickname was designed to conjure images of Alcatraz island, the inescapable maximum-security federal penitentiary which housed actual, notorious criminals. The South Florida Detention Facility ("Alligator Alcatraz") was not a traditional brick-and-mortar jail. Rather, it was an isolated mini-city of large soft-sided tents containing cages where people were confined in inhumane conditions, which has now been closed. But although it is closed, it should not be forgotten.

Family visitation was not allowed, and it was extremely difficult for lawyers to communicate with their clients there. It was overcrowded with little room for people to move. The food was spoiled and maggot-infested. Mosquitoes swarmed and toilets overflowed. Showers were scarce. If the air-conditioning was working, the temperatures inside the tents could be freezing cold. If the air-conditioning stopped working, the heat and humidity made it unbearable. The lights were kept on 24 hours/day, 7 days per week, which was disorienting for anyone incarcerated there. Although there was medical staff present, there were documented reports that detainees were neglected and did not receive proper medical care, resulting in people with pre-existing medical conditions having their health horribly deteriorate because of ICE's disregard.

Unlike the real Alcatraz, Alligator Alcatraz was not filled with the 'worst of the worst' of convicted criminals. Rather, most of the detainees at Alligator Alcatraz only had civil immigration violations but were subjected to some of the worst abuses ever committed by the U.S. government against civilians.

Life Choices

Some officials under the current administration have liked to say about noncitizens in immigration custody, "Being detained is a choice," meaning that the noncitizen is always free to self-deport prior to being arrested by ICE. But a noncitizen who is applying for asylum because they are afraid to return back to their country should not be given a "choice" between two alternatives of either returning to the country they fled for their life from vs. being locked up indefinitely by the United States in an immigration detention center. Both are terrible.

The fact that a noncitizen prefers to remain in an immigration detention center over being sent back to their country of origin should tell you something about how bad it must have been for them in the place they left. And in the case of a noncitizen who has never been arrested for a crime, is in his forties and came to the United States when he was 19, looking for a better life, and now has two kids who are U.S. citizens, that person who is locked up in an immigration detention center is holding on to the hope of being able to live with his children in the U.S., instead of giving up and having to uproot his family to go live in Mexico. These are not "choices" to be in the immigration jail. For these noncitizens, being locked up in an immigration jail is the only option the U.S. government is offering them.

Want to know what is a choice, though? The United States government locking up children is a choice. Since 2025, over 6,200 children have been incarcerated by ICE, including more than 500 babies and toddlers age 3 or younger. At least 1,600 children have been held in custody for longer than 20 days, including at least 175 babies and toddlers who were held longer than 20 days. This is harming children. Families have reported moldy food and undrinkable water, lack of appropriate medical care, and psychological distress. The children suffer from the trauma of incarceration; they will carry this with them for the rest of their lives.

I would ask the U.S. government, "You mean to tell me there are no other alternatives? The government has to lock up the kids? The government has no choice?" Of course, the government has a choice. They could figure something out. The government is making a choice to lock up kids. That's what they are doing. And they need to stop. We need to fix the current immigration laws and make it so that the federal government does not incarcerate children for civil immigration violations. We need to change the law so that children are never put in immigration jail at all, and anyone who is held in immigration custody should be held in conditions that provide for their health and well-being.

ICE previously instituted the Family Case Management Program from 2016 to 2017 to avoid putting families in detention and to help ensure that they attend immigration court hearings. According to reports, the program had a record of 99% court attendance. So, it seems clear that the government can avoid putting children in immigration jail when it wants to. I would propose that ICE reinstitute and expand the Family Case Management Program in order to avoid having any children in immigration jail.

One of most common sense, middle-of-the-road proposals to change the immigration laws regarding detention is the Dignity for Detained Immigrants Act sponsored by Congresswoman Jayapal. This bill would fix the problem that we have now: the presumption that immigrants should be detained. The bill would change the law so that the government could still detain and incarcerate an immigrant, but in order to do so, the government would have to show a good reason that an immigrant should be locked up, such as if the person is a danger to the community or a flight risk.

Under this bill, it would put the burden on DHS to show clear and convincing evidence that alternatives to detention would not work or that the immigrant is a threat to the community. It should be noted that this proposed legislation is actually not an attack on the mere existence of immigration detention centers. This bill would not require that all immigrants be released. Instead, it would mean that there would have to be a good reason to keep someone locked up.

This bill would also make immigration detention resemble due process. For example, if a person is arrested and charged with a crime in criminal court, they are entitled to a prompt hearing with a judge to determine if they should be released on bail (due process). Under this bill, the government would be required to make a written custody decision within 48 hours of arrest, and if the government decides to keep the person in custody, the person would get a hearing with an immigration judge within 3 days. This would go a long way toward fixing the current problem: immigrants being held for months without a bond hearing. The bill would also require detention standards, and a safe environment with adequate medical care. In addition, this bill would dramatically reduce the amount of money being spent on immigration detention. Instead of spending over $150 per day per person to incarcerate them, this bill would use ICE's already-existing Intensive Supervision Appearance Program to ensure that people appear for court appearances, which would only cost about $8 per day per person. In other words, this bill would save the government billions of dollars that don't need to be spent on private prisons.

This bill does not get rid of immigration jails entirely. Government-run immigration jails would still operate, but government contracts with private prisons would be phased out.

Another middle-of-the-road solution that has been proposed is a bill called the "Ban Warehouse Detention Act." The premise of this act is something so obvious it shouldn't be controversial: that the government should not be housing or storing human beings in warehouse detention centers. Again, this bill does not stop all immigration jails. They just can't be warehouses. This is an issue of basic human dignity and sanitation.

Mandatory Bail

I would add an additional modest proposal to change the current immigration laws regarding bail for noncitizens. We should have a clear rule for immigration judges to follow regarding either holding noncitizens under "mandatory detention" (for a serious crime) or releasing them on bail. The immigration law refers to bail as "bond."

Since July 8, 2025, the government has interpreted current immigration laws as giving the government the right to incarcerate all noncitizens who came to the U.S. without a visa, to hold them without bond no matter where they are in the United States and no matter how long they have lived here. What the law actually says, under INA Section 236(a), is that noncitizens who are already present in the U.S. but who are deportable can be either detained or released at the discretion of an immigration judge, while their deportation case is pending. This section allows an immigration judge to grant a noncitizen release on a bond of at least $1,500 or deny bond altogether if the judge thinks the noncitizen is a danger to the community or a flight risk.

To bypass this judicial discretion, the government is relying on Section 235(b), which says that a noncitizen who arrives *at the border* without a visa is subject to mandatory detention. The government has been arguing that noncitizens who entered the U.S. without a visa years ago and have been living in the U.S. should be perpetually considered to still be "applicants for admission" applying to be admitted, as if they are still at the border now, and thereby subject to mandatory detention under 235(b). This distorts the law and violates the Fifth Amendment of the Constitution by taking away their liberty without due process.

This radical policy to incarcerate all undocumented immigrants without bond has led to over 11,000 lawsuits since 2025 where noncitizens have sued the government in federal court, claiming that the government is holding them in custody unlawfully. The noncitizens have won over 10,000 of these lawsuits. It's incredible that, in over 90 percent of the cases, federal courts have ruled that the government has violated the law by unlawfully incarcerating immigrants without bond. In federal court, the government policy has been found to be unlawful by federal judges. The judges who have ruled against the government are not "activist" judges. They are judges of all political stripes, appointed by both Republican and Democratic Presidents, including judges appointed by President Trump himself.

The cost to everyone involved has been enormous. Obviously, this has resulted in incalculable human suffering for the incarcerated immigrants themselves and the toll it has taken on their families, including their kids who are U.S. citizens, because these are noncriminal people who were suddenly arrested and then held without any opportunity to be released.

There is also the cost to the government itself, the federal courts, and taxpayers. The largest self-inflicted cost to the government and taxpayers has been the billions of dollars paid by the government to private prison companies.

Furthermore, the lawsuits have clogged the federal court system, resulting in a strain on federal court judges who have had to decide these thousands of cases. In addition, it has put enormous pressure on government attorneys in the Department of Justice who have had the unenviable task of trying to defend these lawsuits. In a situation where the government has lost over 90 percent of these cases, many of these cases have been indefensible.

The government has spent money defending their indefensible positions in court, and also has had to pay the attorney fees for some of the immigrants who sued. Under the Equal Access to Justice Act, there have been cases where the government has had to pay the immigrants' attorney fees after the government loses the case because the government's actions and legal position were not substantially justified under the law. For any U.S. citizen who is concerned about wasteful spending of taxpayer dollars, it should be alarming that the government has put itself in the position of getting sued over 11,000 times by immigrants and losing over 90 percent of the cases, resulting in the government sometimes having to pay attorney fees.

Many of the lawsuits brought by noncitizens in federal court have been brought because the government denied them even a hearing under Section 236(a). And in some cases, after winning the lawsuit and a federal judge ordering a bond hearing, immigration judges have then denied bond by citing specious reasons to find that the noncitizen is a "flight risk" or a "danger to the community." This has basically been the government trying to unlawfully incarcerate a noncitizen under the wrong statute 235(b), and then when the federal court judge rules against them and says the noncitizen is entitled to a bond hearing, the government makes up some other reason to say the person can't be trusted to go to court or that the person is dangerous.

At some point, the Supreme Court will weigh in and decide if 235(b) authorizes mandatory detention of all undocumented immigrants anywhere in the U.S., as the government contends, or if 236(a) authorizes them to be released on bond.

But regardless of what the Supreme Court does on this issue, we should change the law to reflect what everybody understood for decades prior to 2025, that noncriminal noncitizens inside the United States who might be deportable are eligible for bond. To do this, we should amend Section 235(b) to make clear that it only applies to noncitizens who are either at Ports of Entry or within 50 miles of the border and who have been in the U.S. for less than two weeks. These folks are true applicants for admission who should not be released into the U.S. if they don't qualify to be admitted into the country.

In addition, I propose that for a noncitizen who is deportable but has not been convicted of a serious crime, we should change Section 236(a) and have a rule of "mandatory bail" of a reasonable amount the noncitizen can pay according to their financial circumstances, in an amount between $1,500 and $10,000, to be released from custody, along with the supervised release by immigration authorities to ensure that the noncitizen attends court hearings.

This would still allow the government to hold someone in custody if they really are the "worst of the worst," but would eliminate the current problem of incarcerating nondangerous noncitizens indefinitely.

We can have reasonable laws and standards regarding holding immigrants in custody when it makes sense, such as when a noncitizen has been convicted of a serious crime. But we should end the current practice of incarcerating as many immigrants as possible for no legitimate reasons. It is cruel to them and costly to U.S. taxpayers. We need to enact immigration law reforms that make sense, so that if someone is truly a danger to the community the government can protect the community, but if someone is not a danger to the community and there's no reason to believe they won't attend immigration court hearings, they should be allowed to be out of custody while they attend immigration court.

CHAPTER 14

The Future Looks Bright (With Immigrants)

AMERICA WILL ALWAYS HAVE A bright future with immigrants. If we change the immigration laws to what I have proposed in this book, the United States will do well. As a country, we need to stop dragging ourselves down with the 1996 IIRIRA law and change it to something that will help us achieve our full potential. This book's common sense plan for immigration reform will make America stronger for generations to come. This book can serve as a blueprint for the future of immigration law in the United States.

But before we talk about how great our future will be with immigrants, it's important to take a hard look at the dire consequences of mass deportations—the road we're going down right now. Deporting 10 million immigrants (or more) under the current immigration laws would harm hundreds of thousands of U.S. citizen children whose parents are undocumented. These children are facing the prospect of either growing up in the United States without one or both parents, or having to relocate to another country and be deprived of living in their own country. In addition, deporting all of the currently undocumented immigrants would drastically damage our country economically by diminishing our workforce.

The economic impact on the U.S. of mass deportations is enormous. Let's start with what the University of Pennsylvania economists say. Penn has an organization called the Penn Wharton Budget Model that does economic analysis of fiscal policy without taking sides. In July 2025, they published a report called "Mass Deportation of Unauthorized Immigrants: Fiscal and Economic Effects." They found that if the government carries out mass deportations of all undocumented immigrants over the next 10 years, by deporting 10 percent per year for 10 years (thereby actually deporting all of the undocumented immigrants currently in the United States), it would have extremely negative economic effects on U.S. citizens. Apart from the $170 billion that the government plans to spend to carry out the deportations, it would result in a nearly $1 trillion increase in the federal deficit, because we would have fewer workers, fewer consumers, and lower average wages. The current government policy of mass deportations is shrinking the economy by removing workers. High-skilled U.S. workers would actually make less money without undocumented immigrants being a part of our economy because the more than 10 million undocumented immigrant workers are a complementary part of the economy. That's an economic fact.

We have so many industries that depend on undocumented workers. In the food supply chain industries, there are over 1.5 million immigrant workers who do not have legal immigration status. This includes workers in agriculture, animal slaughtering and processing, packers and packagers, and restaurant cooks and servers. If our government deports all of these workers, who is going to do these jobs? Are there really enough Americans to do this labor?

In the construction industry, approximately 1.5 million workers are undocumented. Texas leads the nation in the number of undocumented construction workers, with approximately 400,000.

Other states with a supersized need for undocumented construction workers include Florida, Georgia, North Carolina, Tennessee, New York, New Jersey, Illinois, Maryland, and California. They are not just laborers, but also plasterers, drywall installers, roofers, painters, and flooring installers. So, when we talk about who is building our country right now, we need to take stock of the fact that Americans are working alongside undocumented workers to get the job done. The National Association of Home Builders has stated that the construction industry already has a shortage of at least 200,000 workers. If the U.S. government were to deport 1.5 million existing construction workers across the country who are already here doing the work, who is going to step in and do those jobs? We don't have 1.5 million native-born U.S. citizens ready to step in and do those jobs. If we did, we wouldn't have a 200,000 worker shortage in the first place. Deporting all of the undocumented construction workers would exacerbate the problem, not make it better. The shortage of workers would be far worse and many projects wouldn't get done. So, if we want to build all the affordable housing we need in this country, we need the help of all the workers who are already here but who are currently undocumented.

In elder care, we already have a shortage of workers, and the need for caregivers is going to increase in the coming years. Right now, there are hundreds of thousands of undocumented immigrants who are currently working to care for older Americans, doing necessary work like bathing, feeding, and physically lifting them. With an aging population, our need for caregivers in the future is sure to increase. We already have a shortage of caregivers, so what are we going to do if we deport hundreds of thousands of the ones we have? If we deport them, we won't have enough caregivers to take care of all our seniors.

Currently, millions of undocumented workers are contributing to Social Security, which means they help fund it. For example, in 2024, undocumented workers paid in approximately $24 billion to Social Security. Penn Wharton has estimated that deporting millions of undocumented workers over the course of 10 years would cost Social Security $133 billion in lost contributions over the course of those 10 years, and then it's a slippery slope from there. They say that over the course of 30 years without those workers, it would result in the loss of $884 billion. In other words, if all the undocumented workers get deported and we don't have their contributions to the Social Security system, it will make it harder for Americans to retire.

But if we stop the madness of mass deportations and pivot to common sense immigration reform, immigrants can continue to work alongside native-born Americans and make America great. We can continue to be able to enjoy bountiful food production. We can have more affordable housing. Americans can continue to count on Social Security for their retirement. The elderly will be taken care of. And we can stop the flow of drugs into the United States through Ports-of-Entry, because the immigrants will pay the United States government enough money to finally achieve 100 percent scanning of all cargo. If we enact common sense changes to the immigration laws, this future can be ours.

Make America Stronger

If we update the Section 249 Registry date to November 3, 2020, as suggested in Chapter 2, we will finally give millions of undocumented immigrants the opportunity to "do it the right way," and the government will receive an immediate benefit of $30-40 billion from restitution payments to pay for permanent border security. The immigrants who are currently undocumented would then continue to pay into Social Security and ensure that we have enough money to pay for Americans' retirement. Updating Section 249 Registry would keep the 1.5 million currently undocumented construction workers on the job, to reach our goal of having affordable housing for ordinary Americans. Registry would also allow caregivers to continue to take care of our seniors. The Farm Workforce Modernization Act would ensure that we can continue to put food on the table. The Essential Workers for Economic Advancement Act would provide visas for temporary nonagricultural workers in areas experiencing labor shortages. With these common sense changes, this bill could dramatically strengthen the United States, both in the short-term and long-term. Just as importantly, Registry would give credence to the family values that we espouse.

Make Immigration Enforcement Smart

We can have strong civil immigration law enforcement without breaking the bank. And we can make it more efficient so that it actually accomplishes its purposes. Registry would give millions of peaceful long-term undocumented immigrants the ability to "do it the right way" and not be vulnerable to senseless deportations. This would save billions of dollars that the government would no longer need to spend to try to deport them. The Real Courts, Rule of Law Act would make Immigration Court a real independent court and not be subject to abuse by the Executive Branch. The Immigration Court could appropriately prioritize cases to eliminate the backlog of almost 4 million deportation cases. The immigration judges could actually take the time to hear asylum claims instead of rushing through them or pretermitting them to deport people to third countries where their lives would be in further danger.

Instead of the government giving a payday to private prison companies by locking up everyone with an immigration violation, we could save billions of dollars by efficiently monitoring immigrants while they attend immigration court. This would have the added benefit of keeping those individuals productive because they could continue to work and take care of their families.

Want to truly get rid of the "worst of the worst"? Repealing the 287(g) program and replacing it with a nationwide Priority Immigration Law Enforcement program will ensure that immigrants who are convicted of serious crimes would be dealt with appropriately, without sweeping in all undocumented immigrants who have any contact with law enforcement. Local police could focus on keeping our communities safe, and not waste their time on civil immigration enforcement against people who are not dangerous.

Enacting the ICE Security Reform Act would ensure that Homeland Security Investigations (HSI) continues its important criminal law enforcement work to protect Americans from transnational crime organizations, human trafficking, and financial crimes. We will still keep the homeland secure.

Recreating the Immigration and Naturalization Service and having new rules for civil immigration law enforcement will enhance public trust. This will ensure that U.S. citizens and immigrants alike continue to enjoy the protection of the Constitution.

Enacting the Dignity for Detained Immigrants Act and the Ban Warehouse Detention Act, along with mandatory bail for noncitizens who have not been convicted of serious crimes, would save billions of dollars that are currently being wasted to incarcerate nonviolent immigrants, and ensure that we treat people humanely.

Finally, enacting the Qualified Immunity Abolition Act and enacting a new federal Anti-Doxxing law would give important civil rights of redress to both victims of excessive force and also to federal agents.

We all need to compromise and come together if we're going to fix immigration in the United States. The plan I have outlined in this book will help Americans enjoy plentiful food, affordable housing, secure retirement, and the security of our nation. Just as importantly, if not more so, we can be a country full of grace, kindness, and compassion. We can re-affirm to ourselves that's who we are. Let's work together to make our future bright.

Call to Action

As a country, we have a choice. We do not have to keep our current immigration laws. We can change them and make it so that the law says an undocumented immigrant who has lived in the U.S. since before November 3, 2020, and has not committed a crime, can apply for legal immigration status. The only reason they can't do it and haven't been able to do it so far is because we have not yet changed the law to make it happen. We can make it happen. I invite you to contact your congressional representatives and ask them to make the changes in this book to finally fix immigration in the United States.

Sources

Introduction: Common Ground

Lincoln, Abraham. "Annual Message to Congress." December 8, 1863. In The Collected Works of Abraham Lincoln, edited by Roy P. Basler, 7:36–53. New Brunswick, NJ: Rutgers University Press, 1953.

But First, How We Got Here

U.S. Citizenship and Immigration Services (USCIS) Historical Library, Origins of the Federal Immigration Service Overview.

Emergency Quota Act of 1921, Pub. L. 67-5, 42 Stat. 5; and Immigration Act of 1924 (Johnson-Reed Act), Pub. L. 68-139, 43 Stat. 153.

Registry Act of 1929, Pub. L. 70-962, 45 Stat. 1512.

U.S. Department of Defense / Center for Military History, Foreign-Born Personnel in the World War II United States Armed Forces Statistical Reports.

Mexican Farm Labor Agreement, Executive Agreement of August 4, 1942; later codified via Act of July 12, 1951 (Public Law 78).

Immigration and Nationality Act (INA) § 245(a) [8 U.S.C. § 1255(a)] and Legal Immigration Family Equity (LIFE) Act Amendments of 2000, Pub. L. 106-554.

Cancellation of Removal: Immigration and Nationality Act (INA) § 240A(b)(1) and § 240A(e)(1) (Statutory annual limit of 4,000 grants for non-permanent residents).

2006 Bill: Comprehensive Immigration Reform Act of 2006 (S. 2611), 109th Congress. Passed the Senate on May 25, 2006.

2013 Bill: Border Security, Economic Opportunity, and Immigration Modernization Act (S. 744), 113th Congress. Passed the Senate on June 27, 2013.

2024 Border Legislation: Emergency National Security Supplemental Appropriations Act (Senate Bipartisan Border Bill), debated February–April 2024.

Bier, David J., Michael Howard, and Julián Salazar. "Immigrants' Recent Effects on Government Budgets: 1994-2023." Cato Institute White Paper, February 2026.

Landgrave, Michelangelo and Alex Nowrasteh. "Illegal Immigrant Incarceration Rates: Analysis of Jan 2025–Jan 2026 Demographic Trends." Cato Institute Immigration Research Briefs. (Confirms native-born Americans are roughly twice as likely to be incarcerated relative to their demographic share).

Noncitizen Voting Audits: Brennan Center for Justice, Noncitizen Voting: The Facts Behind the Myth (Comprehensive multi-election dataset proving statistical insignificance).

"From IIRIRA to Trump: Connecting the Dots to the Current US Immigration Policy Crisis," Donald Kerwin. Center For Migration Studies, July 26, 2018.

The Guardian (May 29, 2025): "Trump administration sets quota to arrest 3,000 people a day in anti-immigration agenda."

Transactional Records Access Clearinghouse (TRAC) at Syracuse University (April 2026 Data): "Immigration Detention Quick Facts."

"5% of People Detained By ICE Have Violent Convictions, 73% No Convictions," David J. Bier, Cato Institute.

"Taking Stock: Trump Administration Record on Detention and Removals," TRAC Immigration.

National Bureau of Economic Research (NBER) / CU Boulder Study (February 2026): "As ICE arrests reach record highs, percent with criminal record plummets."

Brennan Center for Justice Report (Late 2025): "Despite Budget Surge, ICE Fails to Make the Country Safer."

ICE Detention Surge: No Criminal Conviction Cases FY 2026 Data.

Cato Institute Research Brief (Updated March 2026): "Illegal Immigrant Incarceration Rates: The Demographics of American Imprisonment."

"From Private Prisons to Private Detention: Visualizing the Business of Immigration Enforcement," Brett C. Burkhardt, Socius: Sociological Research for a Dynamic World, vo.l. 10 (September 2024).

"What is the daily cost of detaining someone arrested by ICE?" Janet Nguyen, Marketplace, July 25, 2025.

"Who profits from a $45 billion investment in immigrant detention?" Elizabeth Trovall, Marketplace, August 18, 2025.

"How Much do ICE Raids & Detention Cost per arrest?" Alex Pow, Financial Oversight & Policy Research Brief, 2025.

"Does each ICE deportation cost taxpayers at least $17,000?" Brian Arola, MinnPost/Wisconsin Watch, November 19, 2025.

"MISPERCEPTIONS ABOUT IMMIGRATION TO THE U.S: WHAT THE EVIDENCE SHOWS," Compiled by Carola Suárez-Orozco August 15, 2024.

"Immigrants Are Vital to the U.S. Economy," Joint Economic Committee.

Registry

Padilla Legislation: Renewing Immigration Provisions of the Immigration Act of 1929 (S.2606). Introduced by Senator Alex Padilla to transition the Registry framework to a 7-year rolling system.

Statutory History: Immigration Act of 1929, Pub. L. No. 70-962, 45 Stat. 1512; and Immigration Reform and Control Act (IRCA) of 1986, Pub. L. No. 99-603, 100 Stat. 3359 (setting the Jan 1, 1972 benchmark).

"Americans Want More, Not Less, Immigration for First Time," Mohamed Younis, July 1, 2020, Gallup.

Clemency and Pardon Records: U.S. Department of Justice, Office of the Pardon Attorney, Actions on Clemency Requests During the Trump Administration (June 2018 Commutation; August 2020 Full Pardon).

First Step Act: The First Step Act of 2018, Pub. L. No. 115-391, 132 Stat. 5194.

Salazar Legislation: The Dignity Act (H.R. 3599), introduced by Rep. María Elvira Salazar (R-FL).

"How Immigrants and Their U.S.-Born Children Fit into the Future U.S. Labor Market," Jeanne Batalova, Julia Gelatt and Michael Fix, Migration Policy Institute.

The Aggravated Felony Definitions: Immigration and Nationality Act (INA) § 101(a)(43) [8 U.S.C. § 1101(a)(43)].

Inadmissibility and Deportability Grounds: INA § 212(a)(2) [8 U.S.C. § 1182(a)(2)] and INA § 237(a)(2) [8 U.S.C. § 1227(a)(2)].

Historical Origins: Anti-Drug Abuse Act of 1988, Pub. L. No. 100-690, 102 Stat. 4181 (Establishing the initial definition of an aggravated felony).

Dreamers

State of Texas, et al. v. United States (S.D. Tex. 2021) (Judge Hanen's July 16, 2021 memorandum ending new DACA enrollments).

California Senate Bill 960 (Effective Jan 1, 2023).

Illinois House Bill 3751 (Effective Jan 1, 2024).

Colorado House Bill 23-1143 (Effective 2023).

DACA decision: Matter of Santiago-Santiago, 29 I&N 589 (BIA 2026).

The Biden Years

CBP Statistics: U.S. Customs and Border Protection, Southwest Land Border Encounters Enforcement Records (FY2021–FY2024 broken down by Border Patrol apprehensions versus Office of Field Operations encounters).

Darién Gap Data Logs: Servicio Nacional de Fronteras (Senafront) and El Ministerio de Seguridad Pública de Panamá, Informe de Tránsito Irregular de Extranjeros por la Región del Darién.

"Opening Doors, Hardening Borders: Inside Biden's Strategy on Mixed Migration and the Lessons Learned for Europe," Kelsey Norman, Ana Martin Gil. Baker Institute, October 20, 2025.

"Biden administration has admitted more than 1 million migrants into the U.S. under parole policy Congress is considering restricting," Camilo Montoya-Galvez, CBS News, January 2024.

"Biden's Mixed Immigration Legacy: Border Challenges Overshadowed Modernization Advances," Muzaffar Chishti, Kathleen Bush-Joseph, Colleen Putzel-Kavanaugh, and Madeleine Greene, Migration Policy Institute.

Maduro Indictment: United States v. Nicolas Maduro Moros, 1:11 Cr. 205 (AKH) (S.D.N.Y. 2026).

Border Security & New Rules for Asylum

U.S. Customs and Border Protection (CBP) Media Relations, Port of Buffalo Intercepts Over 1,600 Pounds of Illicit Marijuana Hidden in Chocolate Consignment (June 2026).

Truck News (June 12, 2026), "CBP seizes 1,600 lb. of marijuana from truck at Peace Bridge."

The 2021 Law: Securing America's Ports Act, Public Law 116-299 (Statutory 6-year schedule target ending January 5, 2027).

The Core GAO Audit: U.S. Government Accountability Office, Land Port Inspections: CBP Should Improve Performance Data and Deployment Plans for Scanning Systems (Report No. GAO-25-107379, Published September 2025). Documents the omission of the 9 high-volume Southwest ports due to preprimary physical space constraints.

Congressional Correspondence: Senator Maggie Hassan, Official Letter to CBP Leadership regarding Modernization of Vehicle

Non-Intrusive Inspection Tech (June 23, 2026). Cites the February 2025 benchmark of 52 operational systems out of 153 planned large-scale units.

The One Big Beautiful Bill Act, Public Law 119-21 (Enacted July 4, 2025).

The Secure America Act of 2026 (Legislative text defining the $3.45 billion technology and infrastructure funding wall through fiscal year 2029).

The 2025 Reintroduction Bill: House Resolution 4393 (The Dignity Act of 2025), Section-by-Section Analysis, Division A, Title V: Asylum Reform.

National Immigration Forum, The Dignity Act of 2025: Bipartisan Bill Summary and Asylum Overhaul Guidelines (Updated July/August 2025).

Make Immigration Court Constitutional

Case Completion Quotas: U.S. Department of Justice, Executive Office for Immigration Review (EOIR), Memorandum from the Office of the Chief Immigration Judge: Immigration Judge Performance Measures (Implemented October 1, 2018 under AG Jeff Sessions).

The Article I Legislation: The Real Courts, Rule of Law Act (H.R. 6577 / modern iterations), establishing an independent United States Immigration Court system under Article I of the Constitution.

American Bar Association (ABA) Commission on Immigration, Reforming the U.S. Immigration Court System: Executive Summary and Independent Judiciary Proposals.

The Guardian, "US Justice department recruiting legal experts to serve as 'deportation' judges," November 21, 2025.

The 1996 Overhaul Act: Illegal Immigration Reform and Immigrant Responsibility Act (IIRIRA) of 1996, Pub. L. No. 104-208, 110 Stat. 3009-546.

The Hardship Standard and Statutory Cap: Immigration and Nationality Act (INA) § 240A(b) [8 U.S.C. § 1229b(b)] (Defining the "exceptional and extremely unusual" criteria) and INA § 240A(e)(1) (The strict 4,000 annual numerical limitation).

Jurisdictional Regulations: 8 C.F.R. § 214.14 (Allocating sole adjudicative authority over U Visa Form I-918 to USCIS, leaving EOIR judges without statutory jurisdiction).

Backlog Data: Congressional Research Service (CRS) Report, U Nonimmigrant Status (U Visa) Accessibility, Statutory Caps, and Enforcement Overlaps.

Statutory Bond Authority: Immigration and Nationality Act (INA) § 236(a) [8 U.S.C. § 1226(a)] (The core framework detailing general arrest, detention, and discretionary release on bond for noncitizens inside the interior).

Constitutional Precedent: Demore v. Kim, 538 U.S. 510 (2003) and Jennings v. Rodriguez, 138 S. Ct. 830 (2018) (The fundamental Supreme Court templates analyzing the boundaries of mandatory detention without bail under the Fifth Amendment).

EOIR / BIA Tracking: Reference the Transactional Records Access Clearinghouse (TRAC) at Syracuse University (2025–2026 data releases tracking sudden drops in immigration judge counts, rapid closures or reassignments within specific jurisdictions like Northern California, and the dramatic elevation of unrepresented, non-bond detentions).

Kocher, Austin, and TRAC Immigration. "Immigration Court Judicial Staffing Disparities, Removal Order Tracking, and EOIR Case Backlogs." Transactional Records Access Clearinghouse, Syracuse University (2025–2026 Data Releases).

"How Trump Purged Immigration Judges to Speed Up Deportations," Nicholas Nehamas, Allison McCann, Steven Rich, Jazmine Ulloa, and Hamed Aleaziz, New York Times, April 9, 2026.

Interview with Brea Burgie, July 19, 2026.

Temporary Protected Status

Mullin v. Doe, 598 U.S. ___ (6/25/2026).

Ohio Governor's Office News Release June 25, 2026.

TPS Legislative Intent: Senate Judiciary Committee Floor Debates, The Evolution of Section 244 of the Immigration Act of 1990 (Recording the floor statements of Senator Alan Simpson).

U.S. Department of State, Bureau of Population, Refugees, and Migration Tracker of Historic TPS Designations and Terminations (1990–2025).

The Liberian Statutory Precedent: Liberian Refugee Immigration Fairness Act (LRIF), enacted as Section 7611 of the National Defense Authorization Act for Fiscal Year 2020, Pub. L. No. 116-92.

National TPS Coalition Survey Reports, Factual Demographics and Census Profiles of the 1.3 Million Active Status Holders Residing Inside the Interior (March 2025 census audit).

Haitian Workforce Contributions: Center for Migration Studies (CMS), The Economic and Societal Interdependence of Long-Term Haitian Temporary Protected Status Holders Across Essential Infrastructure Sectors.

Optimize Legal Immigration

Farm Workforce Modernization Act: H.R. 1603 (Passed the House in consecutive sessions). Establishes Certified Agricultural Worker (CAW) status, the $1,000 fine framework, and the phased-in E-Verify timeline for the farming sector.

U.S. Department of Labor, U.S. Department of Education, and U.S. Department of Commerce. America's Talent Strategy: Building the Workforce for the Golden Age. Washington, DC: U.S. Department of Labor, August 12, 2025.

Essential Workers for Economic Advancement Act: H.R. 3734 (Introduced by Rep. Lloyd Smucker). Outlines the creation of the temporary H-2C nonimmigrant classification with its baseline 65,000 annual numerical allocation.

Crop Worker Demographics: U.S. Department of Labor, National Agricultural Workers Survey (NAWS) Multi-Year Reports. Tracks the demographic shifts of the agricultural labor pool from the late 20th century into the mid-2020s.

The 140,000 and 226,000 Statutory Caps: Immigration Act of 1990, Pub. L. No. 101-649, 104 Stat. 4978. Establishes the modern layout for numerical limits across family preference and employment tiers.

The Derivative Counting Issue: Congressional Research Service (CRS) Report, Employment-Based Immigration Backlogs and the Asset Allocation of Derivative Family Members.

The 3/10-Year and Permanent Bars: INA § 212(a)(9)(B) [8 U.S.C. § 1182(a)(9)(B)] and INA § 212(a)(9)(C) [8 U.S.C. § 1182(a)(9)(C)].

Minor Permanent Bar Precedent: Matter of Diaz and Lopez, 25 I&N Dec. 188 (BIA 2010).

Same-Sex Marriage: Obergefell v. Hodges, 576 U.S. 644 (2015).

Asylum Definition: INA § 208 [8 U.S.C. § 1158].

USCIS Open Case Tallies: Human Rights First / TRAC Immigration Data Analysis (Tracking the number of active asylum administrative cases through the end of 2025).

Anyone Can Become an American

The Farewell Ceremony: Reagan, Ronald. "Remarks at the Presentation Ceremony for the Presidential Medal of Freedom." Ronald Reagan Presidential Library, January 19, 1989. (This was his final public address as President, where he read the letter containing the famous "become an American" observation).

Official Naturalization Test: USCIS Citizenship Resource Center, Civic Questions and Answers for the Naturalization Test (128 Question Version).

Code of Federal Regulations, 8 C.F.R. § 337.1 (Specifying the exact verbatim script for the Oath of Citizenship and the allowances for religious or conscientious modifications).

Naturalization Act of 1790, ch. 3, 1 Stat. 103; Naturalization Act of 1906, ch. 3592, 34 Stat. 596; and the Immigration and Nationality Act of 1952, Pub. L. No. 82-414, 66 Stat. 163.

The First Amendment

Rumeysa Öztürk v. Department of Homeland Security, et al. (D. Mass. 2025/2026 Settlement Filings).

The Guardian (April 17, 2026): "Tufts University student targeted by administration completes PhD after legal settlement."

Human Rights Watch Policy Document (May 1, 2025): "United States: Repeal the Alien Enemies Act — A Human Rights Argument regarding the March 2025 CECOT Disappearances."

National Immigration Law Center (NILC) Tracker: Tracking the March-April 2025 Wartime Act Removals to the Terrorism Confinement Center (CECOT).

George Retes Jr. v. United States of America, et al., Central District of California, Civil Action No. 26-cv-01290 (Filed February 18, 2026).

Courthouse News Service (February 19, 2026): "Citizen sues ICE over arrest during California cannabis farm raid."

Capitol News Illinois (May 15, 2026): "Ex-residents of South Shore apartment building targeted in massive military-style immigration raid seek millions in damages."

State of Oregon and City of Portland v. Trump, et al., U.S. District Court for the District of Oregon, 106-page opinion issued November 7, 2025 (Documenting the "untethered to the facts" holding).

American Immigration Council Analysis (January 9, 2026): "Can Renee Good's Family Sue ICE in the Aftermath of Her Killing? The Answer Is Complicated."

The 19th News (January 26, 2026): "In Minneapolis, Alex Pretti died as he lived: taking care of others."

CBS Minnesota / WCCO News (January 20, 2026): "Off-duty Twin Cities officers among those 'targeted' by ICE agents looking for proof of U.S. citizenship, chief says."

United States Senate Bill 3625 (The Qualified Immunity Abolition Act of 2026), introduced on February 3, 2026, by Senator Edward Markey and Representative Ayanna Pressley.

Constitutional Protective Baselines: Yick Wo v. Hopkins, 118 U.S. 356 (1886) and Zadvydas v. Davis, 533 U.S. 678 (2001).

Federal Tort Claims Act (FTCA) Law Enforcement Liability Provisions: 28 U.S.C. § 2680(h) (Law Enforcement Proviso) and 28 U.S.C. § 2401(b) (Administrative Presentment Clock rules).

A Plan for ICE

U.S. Citizenship and Immigration Services (USCIS) History Office, The Birth and Evolution of Legacy INS (1933–2003).

The ICE Security Reform Act (H.R. 673 / 119th Congress), introduced by Rep. Robert Garcia (D-CA).

Order of Chief U.S. District Judge Patrick J. Schiltz regarding Non-Compliance and Contempt Threats against Acting ICE Director Todd Lyons, In re: Federal Enforcement Mandates, Civil Action No. 26-cv-00074 (D. Minn., January 28, 2026).

Testimony of Ryan Schwank, Former ICE Attorney and Enforcement Academy Instructor. Hearing on Oversight of the Department of Homeland Security: Safeguarding Constitutional Rights in Federal Enforcement Operations, U.S. Senate Permanent Subcommittee on Investigations, February 23, 2026.

The Washington Post Investigative Report (Late winter 2026 analyzing internal DHS training schedules tracking the drops from 100 days down to 47 and 42 days).

Associated Press (AP) Investigation: Foley, Ryan J. "ICE went on a hiring spree. Sterling credentials were not required, AP investigation finds." The Associated Press, April 17, 2026.

Williams, Reagan, et al. "A Manufactured Crisis": Minnesota Communities Terrorized by the Federal Government. Human Rights Watch, June 18, 2026.

"US: Minneapolis Killing by ICE Unjustified; Shooting a Product of Abusive Enforcement System." Human Rights Watch, January 9, 2026 (Updated January 13, 2026).

The Visible Identification Standards for Immigration-Based Law Enforcement (VISIBLE) Act of 2025 (S. 2212), introduced by

Senators Alex Padilla (D-CA) and Cory Booker (D-NJ) on July 8, 2025.

18 U.S.C. § 119 (Federal criminal code outlining protections for covered public safety and judicial officials against malicious distribution of private information).

House Resolution 8927 (The Stop the Doxx Act of 2026), official press log released by the Office of Representative Josh Gottheimer on June 23, 2026.

Washington State Law: Revised Code of Washington, RCW § 4.24.792.

Klippenstein, Ken. "ICE's Secret Watchlists and Leaked Ledgers: The Multi-Million Dollar 287(g) Law Enforcement Payouts." Independent Report / Document Repository, March 24, 2026.

Institutional Policy Brief: FWD.us Policy Analysis, ICE Financial Ledgers and the Hidden Costs of the 287(g) Task Force Model (Released February/March 2026).

Statutory 287(g) Authority: INA § 287(g) [8 U.S.C. § 1357(g)], created by the Illegal Immigration Reform and Immigrant Responsibility Act (IIRIRA) of 1996.

New Rules for Civil Immigration Law Enforcement

The Interrogation Power: Immigration and Nationality Act (INA) § 287 [8 U.S.C. § 1357].

The Term "Alien": INA § 101(a)(3) [8 U.S.C. § 1101(a)(3)].

The Detainer Standard: 8 Code of Federal Regulations (C.F.R.) § 287.8(b)(2).

United States v. Brignoni-Ponce, 422 U.S. 873 (1975).

Payton v. New York, 445 U.S. 573 (1980).

U.S. Census Bureau, American Community Survey (ACS) Population and Language Characteristics for Los Angeles County.

Pew Research Center, Public Opinion Trends on Civil Immigration Enforcement and Protected Areas.

Agents of Chaos and Cruelty, ACLU Research Report, July 2026.

Kocher, Austin. "The Spatiality of Immigration Enforcement: Mapping the Geography of ICE Interior Arrests and Civil Enforcement Operations." Transactional Records Access Clearinghouse, Syracuse University.

Stop Locking People Up for Fun and Profit

Executive Order No. 9066, 7 Fed. Reg. 1407 (February 19, 1942).

The Ringle Report: Report on Japanese Intel and Loyalty Parameters, compiled by Lt. Cmdr. Kenneth Ringle, Office of Naval Intelligence (1941–1942 text blocks); and personal correspondence from FBI Director J. Edgar Hoover to Attorney General Francis Biddle (February 1942).

Commission on Wartime Relocation and Internment of Civilians. Personal Justice Denied: Report of the Commission on Wartime Relocation and Internment of Civilians. Washington, D.C., December 1982.

Women's Refugee Commission & National Immigration Law Center Data Toolsets (Late 2025/Early 2026 data tracking the 6,200+ minor residential placements and the 20-day detention threshold tracking metrics).

Texas Department of State Health Services, Bureau of Vital Statistics, Coroner's Report on the Custodial Death of Geraldo Lunas Campos.

Foley, Ryan J. "Detention Center Guards Squeezed Life Out of Immigrant, Witness Says." The Associated Press, March 2026.

American Civil Liberties Union (ACLU) of Florida Immigrant Advocacy Project, Inside Alligator Alcatraz: Systemic Human Rights and Health Crises inside the Soft-Sided Tents of South Florida (Published February/March 2026).

Dignity for Detained Immigrants Act (H.R. 2760 / Pramila Jayapal framework outlining the 48-hour administrative clock and the $8 ISAP electronic alternative vs. the $150 bed fee); and the Ban Warehouse Detention Act.

Equal Access to Justice Act, 28 U.S.C. § 2412.

Transactional Records Access Clearinghouse (TRAC) at Syracuse University, Special Report: Federal District Court Habeas Corpus Injunctions and the Interior Bond Crisis (May 2026 Data Release).

"You're Only Getting Out Deported or Dead," Abusive US Immigration Detention at Ft. Bliss, Human Rights Watch, July 15, 2026.

Kocher, Austin, and Transactional Records Access Clearinghouse (TRAC) at Syracuse University. "Immigration Detention Quick Facts: ICE Custody and Conviction Demographics." Syracuse University.

The Future Looks Bright (With Immigrants)

Penn Wharton Budget Model, Mass Deportation of Unauthorized Immigrants: Fiscal and Economic Effects (July 2025).

U.S. Department of Agriculture (USDA) Economic Research Service, Hired Farmworkers Labor Alignment and NAWS Demographic Characteristics Focus.

Center for Migration Studies (CMS), Undocumented Immigrant Workers in the U.S. Economy by Industry Sector.

National Association of Home Builders Economics Group, "Which States and Construction Trades Depend the Most on Immigrant Workers?" NAHB Eye on Housing Analysis, Published April 6, 2026.

Testimony of NAHB Chairman Bill Owens before the House Small Business Committee, Examining Supply-Side Reforms to Close the Housing Gap, May 21, 2026.

American Business Immigration Coalition (ABIC) Policy Brief, Construction: Securing the Workforce Behind America's Growth.

Deloitte and The Manufacturing Institute, Advanced Manufacturing Learning Tracks: Net Positions and the Aging Worker Horizon (2024–2033 Forecasts).

National Academies of Sciences, Engineering, and Medicine, Trends in Global Production Reshoring and Manufacturing Workforce Development Frameworks, June 2026.

The Farm Workforce Modernization Act (H.R. 1603).

The Essential Workers for Economic Advancement Act (H.R. 3734).

The Real Courts, Rule of Law Act (H.R. 6577).

The Dignity for Detained Immigrants Act (H.R. 2760) & Ban Warehouse Detention Act.

The Qualified Immunity Abolition Act of 2026 (S. 3625).

About the Author

ROBERT COUGHLON, JR. was born in 1968, and was raised in southern California. After graduating from the University of Iowa with a degree in English, he attended law school at Whittier College School of Law in Los Angeles.

As a lawyer, he has spent over 30 years working on behalf of immigrants. During this time, he has advised thousands of immigrants regarding the U.S. immigration laws. He has been fortunate to be able to help many people successfully immigrate. But he has also seen how the current immigration laws make it impossible for millions of undocumented immigrants to "do it the right way." He has represented immigrants in family-based immigration, naturalization, removal defense, and federal court habeas corpus litigation.

He is the author of *Fixing Immigration in America*, where he offers a comprehensive plan for how U.S. immigration law should be reformed in a common sense way, and why it would be good for the U.S.

He lives in Phoenix, Arizona.

www.ingramcontent.com/pod-product-compliance
Lightning Source LLC
LaVergne TN
LVHW100730061126
851857LV00011B/474
9798995952411